THE TABLE
OF THE LORD

Published @ 2017 Trieste Publishing Pty Ltd

ISBN 9780649717279

The Table of the Lord by Caroline Fry

Edited by Trieste Publishing Pty Ltd.
Cover @ 2017

www.triestepublishing.com

CAROLINE FRY

THE TABLE
OF THE LORD

Wilson, Mrs. Caroline (Fry)

THE TABLE

OF

THE LORD.

BY THE AUTHOR OF

"THE LISTENER," "CHRIST OUR EXAMPLE," &c.

PHILADELPHIA:

HERMAN HOOKER,

N. W. CORNER CHESTNUT AND FIFTH STREETS.

....

1840.

265.3

876

T. K. & P. G. Collins, Printers,
No. 1 Lodge Alley.

742
W747t

CONTENTS.

CHAP. IX.

CHAP. X.

———

THE LORD'S SUPPER.

CHAPTER I.

ON EXTERNAL ORDINANCES.

God is a Spirit, and they that worship Him must worship Him in spirit and in truth. The bended knee, the sacramental sign, the worded formulary and stated service were not devised for Him. He knows what we want before we ask, and needs not that any man should tell him. He knows what we are before it has been manifested in thought, or word, or deed—before one thought betrays the yearning of our affections—one word confesses the persuasion of our minds—or one act exposes the principle that reigns within us. Nay, the mere voiceless consciousness of the soul is not necessary to Him: He knows our love or hate before it knows itself: He knows—how much! that we have never known, of the heart from which He requires this spiritual worship. "When thou wast under the fig-tree I saw thee."—Saw what? not the man Nathanael in the act, as he probably was, of prayer; this would not have surprised Nathanael into an immediate recognition of his

2

diety. Jesus saw under the fig-tree a chosen
disciple who had not yet known his Saviour,
unconsciously made ready to choose him and
confess him when he appeared. " Rabbi, thou
art the Son of God." All the discovery was
on Nathanael's part; the Master had known
his servant under the fig-tree—and long—how
long before! "Before I formed thee in the
womb, I knew thee."—" According as he hath
chosen us in him before the foundation of the
world." He sees the love that never saw itself,
and accepts the unconscious service. " Lord,
when saw we thee an hungered and fed thee?"
He feels the hatred that knows not its own object: "Who art thou, Lord?" "I am Jesus of
Nazareth, whom thou persecutest." He accepts
the faith that doubts of its own existence—
minute as a grain of mustard-seed; and how he
estimates the guilt of sins unconsciously committed, is apparent in the sacrifices appointed
for them under the Mosaic dispensation.

It is not for Deity, then, that the manifesta-
tions and expression of devotions are required.
It is not for himself God has appointed forms
and places and symbolic signs, nor to himself
he has adapted them. Mark here the pride
and absurdity of human reasoning. We hear
it said, "What does God care for forms and
ceremonies? What can it signify to Him, who
reads the heart, whether I pray in one place or
another, or any where at all, if I live under a

sense of dependence upon Him? Is there any charm in the posture of the body, in the sprinkling of water, and muttering of words, and setting apart of days and sanctifying of places?—Every man is before God what he is in his heart, in spite of creeds, and formularies, and institutions of religion; irrelevant all to the nature of the Eternal Spirit; and what have they to do with the spirit of a man?" We answer, no more than the paper on which our words are written, and the characters in which they are expressed, have to do with the thoughts and feelings they convey from the mind of him who writes, to the mind of him who reads. Religious ordinances are the medium of communication God has appointed between himself and us, suited, not to His nature, but to ours. In earthly language, by material images and with sensible signs, the Deity holds communion with his earth-born creatures, and chooses to receive communications back again. It was left for the intellect of fallen man to discover that they are superfluous, contemptible —to mock at the simple machinery of the forbidden fruit, by which the first movement of sin was to be detected: to cavil at the similitude of earthly passion ascribed to the mind of the impassible God, of joy, and grief, and anger, and repentance; above all, to pour out the full vial of his scorn, the very spleen of his indignant reason, against that great device, that mys-

tery of godliness—God manifest in the flesh.
Were we informed what was the necessity of
submitting Deity to mortal sense, of working
out redemption with material instruments amid
sensible things, rather than in mental and
spiritual abstractions, it might help us to discover why God had joined, and required us to
join, the outward and visible sign of devotion
with the inward and spiritual grace, alone
essential, and alone acceptable to Him. Meantime it is enough for the submitted intellect to
know, that He has so appointed—that He does
so require—and that He accepts, not the ordi-
dances, but our spiritual worship in them: or
rather all in Christ—apart from whom the emotions of the heart and the adoration of the understanding, are of no more value than the flexions
of the knee and the utterance of the lips.

From the beginning God has instituted sacramental signs; material emblems of spiritual
things; memorials and witnesses between himself and man; pledges of promise, and tests of
obligation. Hard by the tree of knowledge,
which tested his obedience, stood the tree of
life, its blessing and reward. The lusting eye,
the profaning hand, transgressing instruments
of the guilt-stirred spirit, should have been
instruments of prevention; for there, within
touch and sight, stood the pledge and emblem
of the life they were to forfeit. Those senses
through which the criminal desire was engen-

dered, when the woman saw the tree that it
was pleasant, should have been the safeguards
of her innocence. Sense was not meant for a
base handmaid to immortal mind; a defence-
less inlet by which the soul's strong hold was
to be betrayed and taken. That opening had
its outworks—it had its own peculiar guard,
and should have tended to the soul's defence.
If the woman had looked upon the other tree,
sense would have helped her to the memory of
God, and all the bliss she was putting to the
venture.

In the great moral dislocation of the fall,
every faculty took its own course of wrong;
one to its pride, the other to its sensuality—
agreed in nothing but to depart from God.
Mind went to war with matter, judgment with
feeling, intellect with sense; what was once
combination, became contrariety, and man was
left at variance with himself; a thing so shat-
tered and broken, that no finite power can
make its parts agree, or fit them once more to
a whole. And thus it is, that while the pride
of reason affects to despise all outward ordinances and visible demonstrations of piety,
feeling is prone to cling to them too much; the
one decries the help that sense affords, the
other loses all spirituality in it. But God, the
wise, the merciful, when he determined to recover and renew his fallen creature, had regard
to each of his dispersed faculties, and suited his

ministration to them all. Those perverted
senses through which the tide of corruption
now flowed in with overwhelming force, sinking the soul in deeper and deeper night, were
not given up by him, to be the exclusive ministers of evil; material instruments, seduced and
seducing as they had become, were not so abandoned, that they should no longer have a voice
to speak for God, or witness of his violated
laws. Indeed when the divine image had de-
parted, and the living soul, having put itself to
·death, proceeded to bury itself in the things of
time and sense, man became so earthly, so ani-
malized a creature, that the ministration of sensible things was found best adapted to his dulled
intellect and blighted feelings. The work of
redemption was begun in signs and shadows of
the things to come: in typical sacrifices and
ceremonial service; every truth was exhibited
under some sensible image, and every promise
ratified by some external pledge. "It shall
come to pass," says the Lord to Moses, after the
most impressive exhibition of his will, with all
the blessing and the curse attached, "It shall
come to pass when the Lord thy God hath
brought thee in unto the land whither thou goest
to possess it, that thou shalt put the blessing
upon Mount Gerizim, and the curse upon
Mount Ebal." We might have thought, that
with all the supernatural evidences with which
they were surrounded, the presence of God upon

the mercy-seat, the Urim and Thummin by
which his mind was known, and all the miraculous interpositions of his power, there could
be no occasion for such memorials to bring to
mind the sanctions of the law, no need of material pledges of his threats and promises.
"Speak unto the children of Israel, and bid
them that they make them fringes in the borders
of their garments throughout their generations,
and that they put upon the fringes of the border,
a ribband of blue; and it shall be unto you for
a fringe, that ye may look upon it, and remember all the commandments of the Lord, and do
them." "How unnecessary! Could they forget the awful sentence that had just been executed upon the transgressor of the law? How
ostentatious! Better write the law upon their
hearts than upon their garments." Some rea-
soners would have said so; just as they say now,
that it is better to be religious in heart than to
make great profession of it, by separation from
the world, observance of ordinances, and attend-
ance upon sacraments. God thought otherwise.
He knew the heart of man—he knew that the
time would come, as it did come to the Jews,
when the divine ordinances would be perverted
and made the substitute for spiritual worship—
when they would make broad their phylacteries
and enlarge the borders of their garments,
while they made the law of none effect through
their traditions. And he knew the time would

come, as it is come to us, when the pride of
man's intellect would revolt against all forms
and institutions of religion, and make a boast
of the spirituality of the gospel, while breaking
its plain commandments in neglecting what has
been ordained. But God yields no more to
man's pride than to his sensuality: they are
equally offensive to him, and equally in opposition to his will. To our weakness only he
has bent himself; to our ignorance he has
adapted the lessons of his wisdom, and to our
imbecility the workings of his power. He does
not require of us now the pure worship of
heaven, but the humble tuitiveness of ignorance
and simplicity: as little children "desire ye the
sincere milk of the word that ye may grow
thereby." He has brought down his high, and
pure, and spiritual religion to the condition of
an earth-born, earth-bound creature, preparing,
but ill prepared as yet, for a sublimer worship.
To help our infirmity, and restrain our licence,
he has most graciously appointed, and through
all time required, external aids and manifesta-
tions of devotion, outward and visible signs of
inward and spiritual grace.

First, the Sabbath; remembrancer once of
the finishing of creation's work; remembrancer
now of the finishing of redemption's harder
work: sweet emblem heretofore of the believer's
rest in Christ; sweet foretaste now of our eternal rest: the Sabbath has been instituted from

the beginning, unchanged as the gracious purpose that ordained it; the blessing of man's innocence, the solace of his fall, the pledge, and
symbol, and means of his recovery. "I gave
them my Sabbaths, to be a sign between me
and them, that they may know that I am the
Lord that sanctify them." One seventh day
the sentence of labor was recalled, the expulsion
from Eden was as it were rescinded, that man
might return and hold sweet communion with
his God; remember what he had been, and be
re-assured of what he will be. But even this
institution, so gracious in the design, so delight-
ful in the enjoyment, so beneficial in its effects;
this dew of heaven on the arid earth, this breath
of immortality in a dying world; even this finds
no acceptance with fallen humanity. Wisdom
disputes it, vice hates it, and independence
treads it under foot. Religion can do very well
without it; and spirituality does not so suffer
under the deadening influence of week-day occupation, as to welcome the refreshment of the
Sabbath service!

Preaching through an appointed ministry, is
another institution that has existed from the
beginning, at least of the economy of redemption. Enoch, the seventh from Adam, prophe-
sied of judgment and of grace to come. Noah,
the second sole progenitor of the human race.
was a preacher of righteousness to his genera-
tion; and throughout the Jewish dispensation,

there were men of God set apart and separated,
to be the oral instructors of his people. "Thou
hast appointed prophets to preach of thee."
Nehemiah vi, 7. "The Lord has anointed me
to preach good tidings," said Isaiah. "Preach
to it the preaching that I bid thee," said the
Lord to Jonah: an office distinct then, it would
appear, from the officiating priesthood of the
temple, and always existing, though peculiarly
characteristic of the gospel dispensation. In
the New Testament, preaching is so specifically
ordained to be the standing means of conversion, is so universally commanded throughout
all times and places, and so manifestly blessed
by the accompanying spirit of God, that it is
only another proof of the rebelliousness of man's
heart, when any can be found to undervalue it:
to say that it does not signify what we hear, or
whether we hear at all: or whether the willing
hearers be supplied with zealous and enlightened preachers, or the appointed preachers be
duly sanctified and fitted for their office; as if
the conduct of the public services and administration of religious rites were all that is essential in the office of a minister. I am sure the
Scripture gives no sanction to such an opinion.
To preach and to baptize is the united commission, and there is no intimation given that
one is of less importance than the other.
"How shall they believe on him of whom they
have not heard, and how shall they hear with-

out a preacher?" As the neglect of the Sabbath has always marked the growth of immorality and irreligion in the world, so indifference to preaching has ever attended the decline of spirituality in the church: and however any man's fancied experience may exalt itself against his Maker's provision for him, I believe the healthful condition of every individual soul is materially affected by the "word preached," as a medium through which God has chosen to communicate with man;—sufficient without it as would be the influence of the Holy Spirit and the written word, had God been pleased to make them so.

A visible external church, in which his name should be professed, his appointed ordinances duly administered, and such order and discipline maintained, as should be suitable to the times and circumstances, was no doubt a very early institution of divine wisdom, for mutual assistance in a spiritual course, and the benefit of each other's gifts and graces. It has been supposed that such a communion is intimated by the casting out of the first open transgressor from the society of God's people. Genesis iv. And more plainly, when in the time of Enos it is said, "then began men to call upon the Lord," perhaps "to call themselves by the name of its Lord;" a professing church openly united for the service of God; a separation rendered necessary by the increasing numbers

of the wicked, and their more open disavowal
of their Maker. However this may be, we
know that God did establish for himself at
length, an outward and visible church, to bear
witness to his name in an idolatrous world,
and exhibit the tokens and emblems of redeeming love; admission to which, by circumcision,
was open to all men, and to his people indispensable.

When these older things were ready to pass
away, the Christian church, with its clearer
light and more spiritual worship, established
by the apostles under the immediate inspi-
ration of the Spirit, took its place. At no
time, as it appears to me, was this external
church identical with the invisible church
of God, although containing it. All were
not Israel who were of Israel; and when we
consider that there was a Judas at the first
administration of the Christian Sacrament; and
many professors in the apostolic church who
walked disorderly, who crucified to themselves
the Son of God afresh, and whose destruction
was sure, I cannot think otherwise of a visible
church, than as the net let down into the sea,
to gather of all kinds, both good and bad, for
the better preservation of the former. Ill indeed does it become us to despise such aid and
encouragement as church-membership affords,
and is by God intended to afford. We may
have our opinion as to where and what is this

external church. I do not think it can be better defined than by the Nineteenth Article of the Church of England. "The visible Church of Christ is a congregation of faithful men, in the which the pure word of God is preached, and the Sacraments be duly ministered according to Christ's ordinances, in all those things that are requisite to the same." If this definition is just, it follows that nothing of man's devising or requiring, however really wise and beneficial, can make or unmake a Catholic church, or hold men of necessity within it, but by the assent of their conscience. However painful to every Christian mind are the separations and divisions upon mere external forms, where all are one in Christ, so sadly characterising the present times, and whatever be the sin of such divisions on any less than conscientious grounds, we cannot presume to say, of any one church exclusively, that it is the church of God, to which men ought to join themselves. But this I think we may say confidently, that they who are careless about uniting themselves with any church, or refuse to communicate with any, because they find none perfect, do set at nought the merciful provisions of God for their spiritual welfare, and despise one of his positive and permanent institutions.

Most beneficent, most necessary, and most imperative upon all men, are the Holy Sacraments, ordained by Christ himself, as a medium

3

of communication between him and us, a means
in which, and through which, his grace may be
received, his salvation commemorated, and his
promises confirmed.   In entering upon this
subject, I feel, and shall feel, through all the
following pages, the tender ground on which I
am to tread.   Truth itself is one—indivisible,
invariable, incapable of difference or diversity.
I cannot think it correct to say of persons who
differ, that both may be right: it is as impossible as that there be more than one right
line between any two given points.   The dis-
sentients may be partially right, or equally
wrong, or there may be no real difference in
the mind, while they differ in expression: or
they may be so far correct, as that contempla-
ting the truth in a different point of view, and
through a different medium, there is, in the
mental vision of each, that which they describe,
though diverse in their statements.   Two ar-
tists drawing from different positions, will produce totally different perspective, and equally
correct: but in that case, neither draws the
object as it is, but as he sees it; and no one
supposes the object to be diverse from itself.
The probability is, considering the weakness of
our comprehension, and the vastness of the
truths to be comprehended; the poorness of
human speech, and the dulness of human hearing, to receive and to convey the mind of God,
the earthly atmosphere through which every

beam of heavenly light must pass, the blindness
of the eye that transmits it, and the perverted-
ness of the mind that finally receives it, the
probability I think is, that while God secures
his own purpose by making the truth sufficiently manifest to every single eye and willing
mind—light still increasing unto perfect day—
no one in this twilight world has so clear and
exact a vision of any thing, as to make those
who differ necessarily wrong; which would be
the case, if any one's conceptions were the perfect truth.   From this imperfection it has come
to pass, that while there are points of revealed
truth, about which the children of God, taught
by one Spirit, are every where agreed, there
have been at all times lesser points, about
which they have differed; or seeming to agree,
would be found to differ, could each produce
the exact impression of his own mind.   Of those
who kneel at the same altar, and break the
same bread, using in perfect honesty the same
form of words—united in one faith, one hope,
one love—members together of one body, even
of Jesus Christ: could each communicant lay
open his impression, feeling, and understanding of these ceremonies, I believe a great diversity of form and coloring would be found,
whilst all are vitally and essentially agreed.
And thus it does always happen, whenever any
one submits to the public eye his own impression of divine truth, he may express himself as

cautiously as he can, some fellow-christian will
be shocked; he may speak as mildly and mo-
destly as he can, some brethren in Christ will
be offended; as moderately as he can, and yet
some tender spirit will be wounded. Perhaps
the reader or the hearer who feels any of these
things, does not always know how deeply the
preacher or the writer feels it too—how often
the fear of man, or the love of man, would
close the lips, or take away the pen, the spirit
shrinking from the collision it anticipates.   I
have no authority to say what a preacher of
the gospel feels; but if I may guess one thing
by another, had he no impulse to obey but
that of nature, were not a necessity laid on
him to preach the gospel of Christ, he would
shrink from the wounds he has to give and to
receive, as much as the coward dreads the field
of battle.

If I proceed with the subject I have entered
upon—if I state what I understand by the
Sacraments ordained by Christ himself; what I
expect when I approach his holy table; what I
mean, when I make use of the prescribed
words, and what I believe and feel when the
rite has been performed; I know that I shall
cross the persuasion of many—I do not mean of
the world, who hold not like precious faith with
ourselves, *that* we expect of course, and intend
no otherwise—but of those who are joined
together in holy communion of the body and

blood of Christ. Some will think perhaps, I fall short of the truth in estimating the design of the Holy Sacraments, or misstate their real nature, or hold myself too free of human authority respecting them: Some I am sure will think I take too lax a view of the right of admission to them, while others may feel that I am too exclusive in the benefits received. Very possibly I may seem to exaggerate, and be the occasion of discouragement to some who have never found it what I may describe. None of this is intended, though it is all foreseen. I write nothing inconsiderately, or as it were at a venture; if any thing is mistaken, it is nevertheless the well-examined, well-established persuasion of my mind, not the mistake of haste or carelessness; if any thing is deficient, or any thing in excess, my error is the communicant's, rather than the writer's: for mine are thoughts, not words; I put down nothing that I have not realised, as I believe in the administration of the holy ordinance. I am induced to write, notwithstanding this anticipation, because I trust that for one who is wounded by the awkwardness of the administrator, many will be healed by the divine truths exhibited; the mistakes will be mine, and the truths will be God's; and I trust that he will bless the one, the other notwithstanding.

3*

CHAPTER II.

ON THE SACRAMENTS.

By consent of all Protestant churches, the Sacraments are but two; and these so directly ordained and commanded by Christ, himself in the New Testament, as to preclude any dispute against their authority, whatever differences may have arisen respecting the nature of them, or the mode of administration. " Go ye therefore, and teach all nations, baptizing them in the name of the Father, and the Son, and the Holy Ghost." "This do in remembrance of me." These two sacraments, therefore, are of divine obligation, and are not left to the choice of any church communion, to adopt or otherwise, neither to the will of any man, to do or to neglect. Although the responsibility of such a neglect will be more fully noticed in a subsequent chapter, we would here observe how lightly this obligation is estimated, as being of God, distinctively, and independently of any human sanctions. That much more deference is actually paid to the authority of man in them, than to that of God, is manifested in stricter observance of the one sacrament, than of the other. Very few parents neglect to have their children baptized: the law of man requires it, and there are civil inconveniences attached to the neglect of it; but many never bring, or care to bring their families to the table of the Lord. Nay, they would not consider themselves Christians, if they had not been baptized: but no man's heart misgives him that he is not a Christian, because he does not, and will not, partake of the body and blood of Christ in the Lord's Supper. And yet the authority is no greater and no less for the one than for the other, nor the command more positive and unrestricted. Most earnestly we would press this reflection upon those, of whom we fear there are many, who take their Christianity for granted, yet never have attended or desired to attend the communion; a communion equally unavailing indeed, with the sacrament of Baptism, to make us Christians: but as professed members of the Christian church, we have never perhaps considered why we attach so much importance to the one ceremony, and so little to the other; placed as they are, on exactly the same ground of benefit and obligation. In many cases the reason ultimately discloses itself; it is the authority of man, and not of God, that is respected in either sacrament. Men will not call us Christians, or give us a decent burial, unless we be baptized; but they will not inquire if we communicate or not; unless it be for some civil purpose enforced by law, in which case we are willing to comply. And thus our very compliance with either ordinance, is shown to be an act of obedience to man, rather than to God, who has appointed both.

The nature and design of the sacraments are more indirectly, but not less surely gathered from the word of God. Our own church thus defines them: "Sacraments ordained of Christ be not only badges and tokens of Christian men's profession, but rather they be certain, sure witnesses, and effectual signs of grace and God's good will towards us, by the which he doth work invisibly in us, and doth not only quicken, but also strengthen and confirm our faith in him." These are indeed the words of man, therefore imperfect, and therefore fallible—to be interpreted by the judgment of man, and accepted or rejected as they shall seem to be in conformity or otherwise with the word of God. But to my apprehension, nothing can be added to make the definition more explicit, or more fully expressive of the divine purpose in the institution of sacramental signs. They are not mere acts of worship, obedience, and acknowledgment on our part, by which we make profession, before God and each other, of the Christian religion. This they are, but not this only. The man who performs either of these rites, does make the profession, and is responsible on his part, and as far as he is able, to fulfil it to the utmost letter of his engagement; how solemnly taken; how deeply obligatory! It does not indeed create the obligation: whatever was due to God after the ceremony, was due to Him before, and would be so though they had never been instituted, or never complied with. This it is most necessary that we bear in mind: because if men do not in argument, they do in their hearts deny it; and from the one sacrament, at least, remain away, lest they make an engagement they do not intend to keep: and probably would do so from the other, were it not performed without their cognizance. Baptism and the Lord's Supper are not arbitrary institutions, to create a relation between God and man which does not exist without them. Every man to whom the word of God has come, is bound to believe in the Father and the Son and the Holy Ghost, to renounce the works of darkness, and become the faithful follower of Jesus Christ, whether in baptism he has promised it or not. Every one who hears the invitation of the gospel, to seek salvation by the blood of Jesus, is as much bound to renounce himself and trust in the righteousness of Christ, as if he had professed to do so at the altar. It was not for himself, to strengthen his own claims, that God appointed these ceremonies: it was to impress them on the memory of his creatures; to convict us from our own lips of the refusal of salvation; to take from us the pretence with which the soul

deceives, and then destroys itself—the pretence
of ignorance; to certify to us the new relationship under which the redemption of Christ has
brought us, by affixing as it were our own seal
to a deed, which is equally valid if we refuse to
sign it. "Say unto them the kingdom of God
is come nigh unto you,"—if they receive you
not, say, 'Notwithstanding be ye sure of this,
the kingdom of God is come nigh unto you.'
Your refusal to make these confessions, vows
and promises, cannot change the case; but they
will be witnesses between God and you, that in
refusing to do so, you openly resist his authority;
or doing so falsely, you confess the truth that
will eternally condemn you, adding the guilt of
a false profession to your other sins. We might
think, of some persons who neglect these holy
ordinances, that they take this last to be the
only damning sin; so heedless are they how
many they commit in their carefulness to avoid
it. In what part of the decalogue do they learn
that hypocrisy is a greater sin than disobedience?
though far be it from us to advise that it should
be added.

But the sacraments are more than badges and
tokens of a Christian profession; they are vows,
acknowledgments and confessions going out
from man towards God. There is a reciprocity
in them. They are witnesses on our behalf, as
well as on God's; they are pledges of His promises, as well as of His claims; they exhibit, if

I may so speak, his signature affixed, as well as ours, to all the engagements of his covenant. Unchangable, eternal love! how little need of this to make thy promise sure, and give security to keep thine own. All is but the indulgence of our weakness—a provision for our mistrust and unbelief—for creatures, who, after all that thou hast done, *can* mistrust thee—*can* forget thee!

Sacraments then, are witnesses and signs, "sure witnesses and effectual signs," in which we may find confirmation and security of God's gracious intentions and good will towards us. When the waters of baptism are sprinkled, we are re-assured of God's faithfulness to his promise, to pour out his Spirit upon all who ask it. When the names of the triune Deity are uttered, we are certified of their eternal covenant to save. When the bread and wine are distributed, it is to confirm the fact of Christ's vicarious suffering, of his body indeed broken, and his blood shed for us. If it be asked, how can such mere ceremonies increase our sense of security, or be any confirmation of the fact; we say, because God himself has appointed them to be so. In condescension to our nature, He has acted after the manner of men, who having agreed upon certain forms of attestation or contract, feel security in the due execution of them: as the scripture speaks—"An oath for confirmation is to them an end of all strife; wherein God, willing more abundantly to show to the heirs of

promise the immutability of his counsel, confirmed it by an oath." The administration of the
sacraments is, as it were, a continual repetition of
this oath in a manner divinely appointed. Heb.
vi, 17. To the end that "we might have strong
consolation who have fled for refuge to lay hold
upon the hope set before us." If they answer
not this end, it is not because we have too much
faith to require such confirmations, but because
we have too little to make use of them.

But more than this, the sacraments are not
only memorials of what God has done, and
pledges of what He intends to do, but they are
the means and instruments by which he does
what he intends; doth "work invisibly in us,
and doth not only quicken but also strengthen
and confirm our faith in him."

The work of salvation, from the first movement of desire in the natural heart to the perfecting of the saint in glory, is of the Father,
through the Son, and by the agency of the Holy
Spirit. Every intermediate means, of which
there are many, is nothing in itself, and nothing
by itself. The tools and instruments which the
Spirit uses to hew the stony heart of man, not
only were useless till He gave them edge and
point adapted to his purpose; but they are useless again as soon as he lays them out of his
hand. I believe that God has not imparted to
any thing, not even to his own precious Book,
an inherent and abiding virtue to communicate

salvation in any of its parts; its beginning, or
progress, or perfection. All are but instruments that He blesses in the using, not that he
has blessed to a perpetual use; for then would
the use be never separated from the blessing,
and the immediate interference of the Spirit
might be dispensed with. It is a necessary distinction; because misconception upon this point
has been a fruitful source of error and confusion, issuing sometimes in the grossest superstl-
tion. When God had appointed burnt-offerings
and oblations, as means through which faith
was to accept and confess the blood of atonement thereafter to be shed, the carnal Jews
believed that the power to take away sin had
been divinely invested in the blood of bulls and
goats; and can hardly now relinquish, when
they become converts to Christianity, the persuasion that some value is continued in these
offerings, though their typical use is at an end.
Again, when God had appointed a visible church
and consecrated ministry to be means of grace
and agents of the Spirit, the Church of Rome
proceeded to think that salvation had been
vested in the church itself, and secured to all
who died within its pale. Protestant churches
have followed the same course: and because
Baptism is made a sign of regeneration, and
when accompanied by the regenerating Spirit, a
seal unto salvation, protestants to no inconsi-
derable extent, have taken the sign for the

4

thing signified, the instrument for the influence
that might or might not accompany it; and at-
tributing to Baptism duly administered an inherent power to regenerate the soul, have determined that every baptised person is a true
Christian and a child of God, born anew of the
Spirit. And though our church gives no countenance to the delusion, we may not be sure
that it pertains exclusively to the Church of
Rome to believe that the consecrated bread,
pressed between the sinner's dying lips, has a
divine charm in it to save the soul. Short of so
gross a superstition, it would be difficult perhaps to trace out the various modifications of
belief in some mysterious influences pertaining
to the Sacraments, inherent and inseparable;
opinions widely distant from each other, and
yet connected by an unbroken chain of error,
through which the Christian church has wound
itself first into, and then out of the doctrine of
transubstantiation. There is no similar confusion in the understanding about common things.
We do not mistake the pebbly bed through
which the water flows for the stream that runs
through it—nor the stream itself for the spring
from which it rises. We seek the water-
course for the water's sake, in places where it
has been used to flow: but we look for the
source of those waters in some distant spring,
which may suspend its issues and leave their
courses dry, and then woe to the traveller who

thinks to drink thereat. Grace flows through
the sacraments, but the sacraments are not
grace. Salvation is by grace, but grace is not
our Saviour. From Him, that eternal source,
the precious waters flow, only so long as He
will pour them out, and only whither He will
please to send them. The sacraments are the
channels by which His blessed influences are
wont to run, and thither He bids the thirsty
come and drink, but they are nothing more.
They are not means of salvation; and if they
were, the believer has no need of them; he
wants no salvation but the sufficient blood of
Christ; and no means to an end that was
accomplished when Jesus "made an end of
transgression, nailing it to his cross,"—when
He said, "It is finished," and gave up the ghost.
But they are means of that which we want
always—of which the more we have, the more
we desire the increase, and fear the diminution;
of which the supply of yesterday is no sufficiency for to-day, nor provison for to-morrow: they are the means of grace. Not only,
as I conceive, are the sacraments outward and
visible signs of inward and spiritual grace; for
the sign or symbol of a thing does not imply
the presence of the reality; but they are very
frequently the means and instruments in the
hand of the Spirit, by which the inward and
spiritual grace is conveyed from God into the
soul of man; whether the first gift of the Spirit

for the conversion of the sinner, the new birth unto righteousness exhibited in Baptism; or the fruit of the Spirit to the perfecting of the saint, sanctification unto life eternal, more properly pertaining to the Lord's Supper. This value, it is true, the Sacraments have in common with all other means of grace ordained of God; such as preaching, prayer, and reading of the word. And yet there seems to be something special in them, as appointed and blessed to a distinct and special purpose: the one, to set the seal of adoption upon those whom God has chosen to eternal life, separating them from an ungodly, unbelieving world; as circumcision was heretofore 'the partition wall which separated Israel from the nations of the Gentiles; the other to be the food and nurture of his adopted ones within their Father's house; as heretofore the manna fell within the sacred precincts of the camp, or more exactly as the paschal-lamb was distributed to all who by circumcision had been brought within the line of separation. The one sacrament exhibits Christ, and when made efficacious by the Spirit, conveys Christ, as the principle of life, or rather life itself, to the soul that was aforetime dead; the other exhibits Christ, and if duly and worthily received, communicates him, as the aliment and sustenance of the life he has imparted; not figuratively, but verily and indeed taken and received in the due administration of it. Still, I think whatever is special in the sacraments, as distinguished from other means of grace, must be looked for in the special blessing likely to accompany ordinances so appointed, and not in any power vested in them to convey the blessing, different from what pertains to other means of grace: since not only are the sacraments continually performed without their effects; but these effects are as frequently, without the sacraments, produced by other means. In the apostolic age, I imagine the regeneration of the soul, and its conversion to the faith, took place before the rite of baptism was performed: whereas now, I suppose it much more frequently takes place in after life. And with reference to the Lord's Supper, we know that the spiritual feeding of the believer upon Christ, is not peculiar to it: but may be realized as well in the most secret communion of the soul with the Beloved. The word of God, and prayer, and preaching, are equally appointed to these ends, and as frequently blessed to the effecting of them. In short, they are altogether nothing—absolutely nothing, but the two-edged sword, which the Captain of our salvation has wrought and burnished for himself, by the right hand of his power, his all-conquering Spirit, to separate his people from the world and force a way for them to glory. He takes it up when He will, and lays

4 *

it down when He has done with it; and it lies cold, and motionless, and useless, till He works with it again; for it cannot be weilded by any mortal hand.

And if mortal hands have no power to give efficacy to the holy sacraments, it is manifest they can have none to take the efficacy away; therefore I think our church has most wisely determined, that while the unfit communicant, being duly warned and instructed, takes upon himself the whole condemnation of his false profession, so also the ungodly minister must bear the iniquity of his profanation, but cannot convey pollution to the sacred rite that he administers. "Forasmuch as they do not the same in their own name, but in Christ's, and do minister by his commission and authority, we may use their ministry both in hearing the word of God, and in receiving of the sacraments. Neither is the effect of Christ's ordinance taken away by their wickedness, nor the grace of God's gifts diminished from such as by faith and rightly do receive the sacraments ministered unto them; which be effectual because of Christ's institution and promise, although they be ministered by evil men." It is a feeling very natural, to like to have these solemn rites performed to us by a righteous man; and inasmuch as they are accompanied with prayer, and "the prayer of a righteous man availeth much," it may not be an unreasonable satisfaction; but we should be cautious of attaching an undue importance to this, as if the most hallowed hand could add any thing to the value of baptismal grace, or of the sacramental emblems of the body and blood of Christ. Neither should we suffer our conscience to be distressed, and our faith disturbed, or as has been sometimes done, forego the ordinances altogether, because they are administered by unrighteous hands. If these divine rites themselves are nothing, but by the present blessing of the Lord, how much less than nothing is the earthly hand by which they are presented, and impotent to bring that blessing or prevent it. "Who shall bless what God has not blessed? and who shall curse what God has not cursed?" Our insufficient value for the precious blood of Christ, and all the power of his death, is in no way more disclosed than by the undue importance we attach to incidental circumstances, connected with the outward administrations of religion or the inward reception of it in our hearts: to form and discipline on the one hand—and to mere frames and feelings on the other; as if the power of His infinite and all-sufficient merit could suffer diminution or augmentation by the machinery made use of in its application to the soul: an unconscious pharisaism very hardly surmounted even in the bosom of the believer, who thinks that he is trusting Christ alone; but very, very seldom realizes the sufficiency and security of what he trusts.

CHAPTER III.

THE Jewish festival of the passover is considered to have been the type and parallel of
the Christian sacrament of the Lord's Supper,
as circumcision was of that of baptism. No
uncircumcised person could eat of the paschal
lamb; and no Christian churches, I believe, administer the sacrament to one who has not been
previously baptised. To the rite of circumcision
there was no exclusive limitation; the heathen
captive or servant bought with money, or any
stranger dwelling in the land, might enter the
Jewish church by this ceremony, and thus
become entitled to its external privileges. (Exo-
dus xii.) "One law shall be to him that is
home-born, and unto the stranger that dwelleth
among you." No qualification is mentioned as
necessary to admission, but that of desiring it,
and nothing is specified as an exclusion to those
who did so desire. "When a stranger shall
sojourn with thee and will keep the passover to
the Lord, let all his males be circumcised, and
then let him come near and keep it; and he shall
be as one that is born in the land." To the
chosen people of Israel no choice was allowed.

"Every man child among you shall be circumcised. It shall be a token of my covenant betwixt me and you." Herein we have election, but not exclusion. In the feast of the passover there was an exclusion; no one could partake of it unless he made an open profession of the Jewish religion by the initiatory rite of circumcision; the outward sign of separation between the people of God and the nations of the world: "For no uncircumcised person shall eat thereof." It hence appears that the one ordinance being designed for all who desired to become members of the church of God; the other was especially reserved to those who already were so. On his chosen people they were equally imperative; for it is said of the passover as of circumcision, that they who partook not of it at the set times should be cut off. Both these rites were a portion of that ceremonial law which, with all its terrors and penalties, has been done away. In tracing the analogy between them and the Christian Sacraments, by which they have been superseded, not continued, we must be careful to keep this in mind, lest we bring ourselves into bondage. The law had a shadow of good things to come, but not, as we have, the very image of the things as they have since appeared. The whole of these shadows passed away together, when more spiritual ordinances were substituted for them. We shall bring great confusion into our minds if we suppose that

some part of the figurative and typical dispensation remains in force, when the rest has passed
away. The doctrines of the Jewish church
remain for ever, for they are one with ours:
there has from the beginning been but one religion; the one only Gospel of our Lord and Saviour Jesus Christ. We cannot drink too deeply
of their molten sea, or feed too often on their
paschal Lamb, or follow too closely the spirit of
their sacrifices. But the forms and ceremonies
ordained for the foreshowing of the Gospel, become mere superstitions if engrafted on the New
Testament dispensation. The word of God
makes no exception when it declares that these
things are passed away. In this view, and in
comparison with the more spiritual exhibition of
the gospel, the apostle calls them " carnal ordinances, beggarly elements;" and such they had
become; for God had done with them and rejected them; though once they had been divine
and holy institutions. The Church of Rome, I
apprehend, has derived no few of its superstitious practices from the Jewish ritual: as the
apostle foresaw, when, cautioning the Colossians
against some of the most prominent superstitions
into which that church had fallen, he says, " Let
no man judge you in meat or in drink, or in respect of an holy-day, or of the new moon, or of
the Sabbath days, which all are a shadow of
things to come—but the body is of Christ."
We derive our authority for Christian ordinances

from the New Testament exclusively: and appeal to the older things as illustrative of our
Sacraments, only so far as they are recognised
in the New Testament to be analogous: by
drawing the comparison closer than is intended,
we should be in danger of inducing legal dependence or superstitious dread. With this in
mind, we may observe, that circumcision and
the passover, beside being outward and visible
signs of inward and spiritual grace, in the manner of our sacraments, were also types and shadows of those very sacraments, and in that character exhibited their nature and design; whence
much spiritual instruction may be expected from
the consideration of them. Our subject confines
us to the passover, in its likeness and relationship to the Lord's Supper.

The Jewish passover, the first great yearly
festival, was commemorative of the deliverance
of Israel from Egyptian bondage, and the sword
of the destroying angel—prefigurative of spiritual redemption by Jesus Christ, the Lamb slain
from the foundation of the world in the purpose
of Jehovah, and actually to be slain on earth
when the fulness of time should come. The
Christian, Sacrament of the Lord's Supper is
simply commemorative of this last event;—" to
show forth the Lord's death till he come:" for
the continual remembrance of the sacrifice of
the death of Christ, and of the benefits which
we receive thereby. The ceremonies peculiar

to the passover, distinguishing it from other festivals, were the slaying of the Paschal Lamb, the eating only of unleavened bread, and the waving of the sheaf of first-fruits on the morrow after the feast. The Paschal Lamb is the universally-acknowledged type of Jesus Christ. The New Testament recognises the similitude. "Ye are redeemed with the precious blood of Christ, as of a lamb without blemish and without spot: who verily was fore-ordained before the foundation of the world, but was manifest in the last times for you." 1 Peter i, 19.

The blood of the slain lamb was not to be spilt on the ground, but gathered in a basin as a precious thing; no doubt to signify the value of that which the Scripture calls the precious blood of Christ, 1 Peter i, 19, but which the unbeliever rejects, and would make to be shed in vain —"eating and drinking their own damnation, not discerning the Lord's body." The typical figure was probably in the mind of the Apostle when he says, "They have trodden under foot the blood of the covenant." Heb. x, 29. It was sprinkled with a bunch of hyssop on the lintels and door-posts of the houses, in memory of the night when the destroying angel turned his sword from every habitation on which the blood was found; typically for the sake of the slain lamb, and the blood of sprinkling, really for the sake of Him who is the substance of the shadow; a beautiful figure of the atone-

ment, in its application to the soul by faith.
The angel of destruction has gone, and goes
continually, and at the last day will go finally,
through every land—through the living and the
dead—he makes but one distinction—acknowledges but one mark. Is the blood of the
paschal lamb upon the door, or is it not? Has
the blood of Christ been sprinkled through faith
upon the conscience, or has it been neglected
and trodden under foot?

The eating of the paschal lamb signified our
spiritually feeding upon Christ by faith, and
sacramentally in the Lord's Supper. As Christ
is therein to be received, "not unworthily," so
in the passover, all was to be done in a prescribed order. They were to eat it standing,
with their staves in their hands, their shoes on
their feet, and their loins girt, a posture of
action, as those that go a journey. Though
this circumstance might be peculiar to the first
passover, it is strikingly figurative of the position of a believer in the Egypt of this world,
from whose judgments he is to be exempted,
and whose bondage he is to escape. It calls
immediately to mind the language of the Gospel,
"Gird up the loins of your minds." 1 Peter i,
13. Be ready to act, to follow—"To follow
the Lamb whithersoever he goeth." " This is
not our rest:" however we be fed and pro-
tected by the Lord our passover, and strengthened and refreshed by the sacramental emblems

5

of his body and blood, we take them as the
traveller takes his fare—prepared for departing
—"Here we have no abiding city, but we seek
one to come." Heb. xiii, 14.

The passover was eaten with sour and bitter
herbs. Christ is fed upon with many a bitter
thought of sin, and many a painful remembrance of His sufferings on our behalf. Repentance and godly sorrow are ever mingled
with the sweet exercise of faith and love, and
are indispensable to the due receiving of the
Christian communion. Perhaps it was thus intimated also that we have a cross to bear before
we reach our crown, and cannot reign except
we suffer with him. They ate it with leaven—
seven days afterward they might eat no leaven.
The New Testament gives us the interpretation
of this, " Purge out the old leaven, and let us
keep the feast with the unleavened bread of
sincerity and truth." 1 Cor. v, 7. " Let us
keep the feast, not with the leaven of malice
and wickedness." 1 Cor. v, 8. Falseness in
principle and wickedness in the life, are the
leaven with which our passover must not be
eaten; the infecting, souring, corrupt admixture,
which will make the spiritual food unavailable,
and the sacramental bread a condemnation.
For seven days: the scripture emblem of a com-
pleted period—to us the completion of all time.
We must eat no more leaven, after partaking of
the body and blood of Christ, "Resolve to lead

a new life." Walking henceforth in his most
holy ways. "Serving the Lord in holiness and
righteousness all the days of our lives."

The whole of the lamb was to be eaten. We
must take Christ and the salvation of Christ
entire. "We do not presume to come to this
thy table, O merciful Lord, trusting in our own
righteousness." We are not at liberty to receive a part and reject a part; to feed upon
Christ for pardon, and upon ourselves for righteousness; to trust his death and our own merits
jointly; nor yet to accept the security of his
redeeming blood, and refuse the sanctifying influences of his Spirit. We are not at liberty to
receive the doctrines of Christ and neglect his
precepts; neither to receive his precepts and
reject his doctrines.

The whole family were to eat it, or if too
small, more than one family together, indicating that this festival, like the Lord's Supper,
was an act of social worship and church communion; the whole church of Christ being one
family, and one body in him. Our church has
recognised this character of the sacrament, as
being a social, not a private act of devotion, by
requiring that it shall not be administered unless
a sufficient number of persons are assembled;
"that is, except four, or three at the least, communicate with the priest;"—it is to be a public
celebration among the living, not a mysterious

ceremony performed in the lonely chambers of
the dying.

Lastly, the passover, as before remarked, was
allowed to no uncircumcised person. The mark
of church-membership, like every thing else in
the Jewish ordinances, was an external one: for
it does not appear that any test was required of
the state of mind of the recipient. This is in
perfect accordance with the whole typical institution. The adoption of Israel according to the
flesh, was a figure of the adoption of grace; not
a figure of the world at large, or the external
church, in which are the godly and ungodly
mixed, but of the invisible church of Christ, the
elect of God, chosen of him and precious. In-
dividually, an Israelite of the circumcision,
might or might not be of the family of Abraham, according to the faith; but they were all,
as born of Abraham according to the flesh,
members of the typical election, and as such
entitled to partake of the typical privileges of
that church. Now, like the true church of
Christ itself, the mark of adoption is spiritual
and not always discernible to the eye of man.
But the exclusion is really as distinct and positive as it was formerly: none but the circumcised in heart, the true believer, can spiritually
eat the flesh and drink the blood of Christ.*

* The above illustration of the passover is principally
extracted from Mather on the Gospel of the Old Testament.

Such was the signification of the Jewish
passover, and such the resemblance it bears to
the Christian ordinance of the Lord's Supper;
pointing, the one forward, and the other backward, to the same event; and both to the
benefits we receive thereby. No mention, I
believe, is made of the passover in the New
Testament after the death of Christ; from which
we may infer that no Hebrew converts to
Christianity continued to keep it; and if some
erroneously did so, it was among the things
against which St. Paul remonstrates when he
says, "Why, as though living in the world, are
ye subject to ordinances?" Again, "How turn
ye again to the weak and beggarly elements
whereunto ye desire again to be in bondage?
Ye observe days, and months, and times, and
years. I am in doubt of you." The substance
had come, and the shadows had passed away:
Christ had died, and the Christian commemora-
tion of his death had been instituted by himself
in the last supper. The memory of the former
things is alone left for our admonition, upon
whom the ends of the world are come. We
turn from the shadow, to contemplate the very
image of these things; of the mystery of redemption.

The narrative of the Last Supper is given
with very little variation by three of the evangelists, the blessed partakers of the holy feast; to
which, if we add the account of the apostle,

who not being an eye-witness, received it from
the united, and by that means more perfect testimony of those who were so; or rather, as he
himself declares, 1 Cor. xi, received it of the
Lord, we shall have all the testimony the
Scriptures afford respecting the first institution
of the ceremony, and the design and application
of it to the church for ever.

Matt. xxvi, 17. "Now the first day of the
feast of unleavened bread the disciples came to
Jesus, saying unto him, Where wilt thou that
we prepare for thee to eat the passover? And
he said, Go into the city unto such a man, and
say unto him, The master says, my time is at
hand; I will keep the passover at thy house
with my disciples. And the disciples did as
Jesus had appointed them; and they made
ready the passover. Now when the even was
come, he sat down with the twelve, and as they
did eat, he said, Verily I say unto you, that one
of you shall betray me. And they were exceeding sorrowful, and began every one of
them to say unto him, Lord, Is it I? And he
answered and said, He that dippeth his hand
with me in the dish, the same shall betray me.
The Son of man goeth as it is written of him:
but woe unto that man by whom the Son of
man is betrayed! it had been better for that
man if he had not been born. Then Judas,
which betrayed him, answered and said, Master, is it I? He said unto him, Thou hast

said. And as they were eating, Jesus took
bread, and blessed it, and brake it, and gave it
to the disciples, and said, Take, eat, this is my
body. And he took the cup, and gave thanks,
and gave it to them, saying, Drink ye all of it;
for this is my blood of the new testament,
which is shed for many for the remission of
sins. But I say unto you, I will not drink
henceforth of this fruit of the vine, until the
day when I drink it new with you in my Father's kingdom. And when they had sung an
hymn, they went out into the mount of Olives."
The only variation from this narrative is, that
St. Luke introduces at the supper some conversation that the other evangelists give as
having passed afterwards; and St. John, omit-
ting the sacramental ceremony altogether,
enters into other particulars of the deepest
interest, by which light is indirectly thrown
upon its mysteries. Let us dwell long upon
this sacred narrative; let us consider, and re-
consider these divine words; the time, the
company, the circumstances that attended it,
and the events that followed. It will be a better preparation for the holy sacrament than any
thing that man can write, or churches dictate.
To those who, for the first time, are preparing
to receive the communion; to all who still think
some peculiar preparation necessary, or are
wishing for some better understanding of it before they go, I would say, " This do; read these

inspired narratives, one or all, with the apostle's
repetition in the epistle to the Corinthians; read
them, sentence by sentence, word by word,
with close meditation and internal prayer;
think them, pray them, over and over again;
that so, by the Spirit's help, your minds may be
enlightened, your hearts made ready, or your
fears allayed. All that we can say to help each
other, all that the wisdom of the church can
add for the instruction of her members, is but
a draught from this pure source; it is worth
nothing unless it was drawn thence. The
Spirit itself will not teach us apart from the
written word. His light, which fell direct upon
the souls of them that wrote it, now comes to
us reflected from its pages. God does permit,
and does intend that we should take advantage
of each other's gifts, and inquire of these who
are before us, to be encouraged by their experience, and warned by their mistakes, and persuaded by their example; but as all human instruction must be brought to the test of Scripture
before it can be relied upon, we shall do well to
begin where our teachers themselves began.
We had better study fully the written word of
God upon the subject of the sacrament, before
we appeal to the opinions of men, or consider
the formularies prepared for us to use. And
may the light of God be with us while we attempt it!

. "When the even was come." "The same

night in which he was betrayed," the last evening of the Saviour's life, the last hours before that midnight, in which the Son of God was given into the hands of sinners, to do with him what they list; the moments immediately preceding the intensest anguish of his soul. How should we wish to know, if we did not know, what occupied that evening! If we have had a friend, a brother, who has died away from us, do we not inquire with intensest interest, what passed in the closing hours of life? what he did last, before the agonies of death withdrew his attention from external things? His latest care, his final conversation, whom did it regard, and what was it about? Do we not know the thrill of sensibility with which we hear, or wish to hear some reference to ourselves, in the dying accents of one we love? The Saviour's last care, his latest occupation before he entered the final conflict with the powers of darkness, was to dictate words for us—to establish for us a sacramental rite—an external ordinance, a ceremony—can we believe it? which we neglect or perform with indifference, or perhaps have never yet performed at all. It was no time to be occupied with things indifferent, with a matter that does not signify, in which we may do as we like, something that can safely be put off or let alone. If Satan has ever told us so, let this question sink deep into our hearts, Was it a moment for the Son of God to occupy himself with what it is not necessary for Christians to observe?

"He sat down with the twelve." It is well to consider who the guests were, that we come not uninvited to the feast, neither think ourselves excluded without cause. The twelve had confessed the man Jesus to be God and Lord; the Messiah that was to come, the Saviour of mankind, as far as the light of their own Scriptures had revealed him: and this they did in opposition to the rejection of him by their people, and the mystery of his humiliation, which they in no wise understood. Chosen by the Saviour when they knew him not, and called to follow him they knew not whither, by faith they obeyed the call, they believed his words, they trusted his promises, and gave up all that they had for his sake. This is their own appeal, "Behold we have forsaken all and followed thee." Every accepted, every welcome guest at the Lord's table, makes a similar confession, is in a similar position. Chosen of God, and called by his Spirit out of a world that lieth in wickedness, they have devoted themselves to be the followers of Jesus Christ, they believe him, they trust him, and forsake whatever would interfere with their devotion to his service. It is the profession required of all who approach the altar, and we are admitted upon our profession, to a feast of which, nevertheless, we can be no partakers, if it be a false

profession: there was one at that first communion who received no benefit thereby.

But the eleven—were they sinless guests?
were they strong in the Spirit, and matured in
faith, and entitled by their holy lives, and undi-
vided hearts, to a participation in the feast?
Were they ready to follow their master to prison
and to death? They said so, and they meant
it, for their hearts were single, and their love
was true; but it did not prove so; twelve hours
had not passed before one denied his master,
and the rest forsook him. It is for sinners, then,
miserable sinners, that this feast was instituted;
for the weak in faith, for the untried in love, for
the uncertain in conduct, for those who had no
strength, no constancy, no faithfulness in themselves, to follow their Master for a single day.
Jesus knew this, but he did not refuse them: he
did not desire them to wait, as we think fit to
wait, till they were holier, and stronger, and
surer of themselves. He gave them the bread
and wine to strengthen and refresh their souls,
that they might grow thereby into that which
they did afterwards become, devoted, sanctified,
and able indeed to follow him to prison and to
death, as several of them did in after-times. It
does not appear that he withheld it even from
Judas. Judas made the same profession as
others of the twelve; he seemingly obeyed the
call to follow Christ, and ranged himself among
his chosen ones: most probably he sinned

against his own conviction that Christ was indeed the Son of God, preferring this world's gain before him. Only to the Master were the secrets open of the traitor's heart: one whom he had chosen was a devil, that the Scriptures might be fulfilled. He kept the secret, and suffered him to pass as his disciple, and as such administered to him the outward and visible signs ôf the communion, the bread and wine, no verity, by his false heart received, of the inward and spiritual grace.

The administration of the Sacrament to all who profess and call themselves Christians, without any satisfactory knowledge of their hearts, has been an occasion of much controversy and separation in the churches. Tender spirits have been deeply pained, and some have even excluded themselves from our communion, because they feared to administer or to partake the sacred emblems, with those who give no token of being members of Christ, and children of God, although baptized to be so. Our church has been much questioned upon this subject, and other churches have devised various .plans to keep their communion pure. It appears to me that the scruple is unnecessary, as the precaution is unavailing. It must be unavailing, because when all is done that can be devised, to test the faith of the communicant, and discover the seal of adoption upon his brow, he may deceive us, if not himself: the

life and conversation have as often denied the
public examination or written experience, as
the renewed baptismal vow; which alone our
church requires. Since after every precaution,
the profession must be taken, I do not perceive
why the mode of profession accepted in our
church, is not as sufficient as any other. The
most powerful exhortations are made, and the
most awful warnings given; a form of words is
prescribed, which no unfit communicant can
speak with truth. A confession of faith or profession of Christ, could hardly be devised more
full and close, than that which every communicant is required to utter before the elements are
delivered to him. What can man do more than
leave the forswearer to his peril? It was what
Jesus did as man, though as God he saw
through all. To show that he was not de-
ceived, he exposed the traitor's guilt at the very
time of the celebration; in one gospel it is said
just before, in the others just after, the distribution of the bread and wine. Judas was not left
to believe, that the bread was blest to him,
although he ate it; nor the wine, although he
drank it; nor we, that he derived any benefit
from them, administered though they were, by
the Lord's own sacred hands. If this administration seems to exonerate the church, that,
giving the impenitent sinner due warning of his
peril, accepts his profession, and leaves him to
the judgment of the Almighty, it places in an

6

awful light the delusion of that church which
attaches to the elements a saving efficacy administered in the last moments of a sinful life.
It was the very moment of the hypocrite's ex-
posure: it was the consummation of his guilt,
that, ready in his heart to betray his Master, he
sat down as a disciple at his table. It was the
time when Satan took full possession of his soul,
to make what use of him he would. Did this
never happen but once? or has the viaticum of
the Papist, and the superstitious reception of the
Protestant bread and wine upon the death-bed,
passed other souls into the hands of him whose
wages they have taken while they lived.

"And as they were eating." The first communion was taken in a sitting posture, after the
ordinary manner of sitting at meat, whence
some Christians have made it a point of conscience, and even a ground of separation from
the church, to take the Sacrament in that position. Certainly there is no reason apparent
here, why we should not take it sitting: but it
seems a trivial question; kneeling is the posture
of devotion, and best becomes the position of
the soul at such a time. The Protestant kneels
to him whom he addresses, but he makes no
address to the elements, as that God were present in them: therefore his position cannot be
construed into an act of idolatrous worship.

"Take, eat, this is my body." In the words
addressed by our Saviour to the disciples, there

is a very slight variation between the Evangelists; but as we have in the epistle to the Corinthians the Holy Spirit's exposition of the ceremony, the variation presents no difficulty. St. Paul says he has received it of God—" That the Lord Jesus, the same night in which he was betrayed, took bread, and ᵢwhen he had given thanks, he brake and said, Take, eat: this is my body, which is broken for you: this do in remembrance of me. After the same manner also he took the cup, when he had supped, saying, "This cup is the new testament of my blood—this do as oft as you drink it, in remembrance of me." Where can we learn the nature of the Sacrament so well as in these few words? How dissipate our fears, or warm our hearts to love, so well as in the meditation of them?

"Take, eat." But were they prepared? were they fit? Jesus did not ask them that; he had not told them to prepare themselves. He had chosen them to be his disciples, and they had chosen him to be their Lord—their right to come was his invitation to the feast, and their title to partake of it was his command. " Take, eat—take what I offer you—eat what I have prepared for you." " Ho! every one that thirsteth, come ye to the waters, and he that hath no money let him come and buy; buy wine and milk without money and without price."

" Take, eat—this is my body." We will not

dwell on the errors of a corrupted church, for
which the only scriptural pretext is derived from
these words—" This is my body;" as if it were
not the commonest phraseology of the inspired
language, to give similitude the form of fact, and
call the emblem that which it represents. " I
am the vine—ye are the branches." " They
drank of that spiritual rock that followed them,
and that rock was Christ." In the language of
our Church—" To such as rightly, worthily, and
with faith, receive the same, the bread that we
break is a partaking of the body of Christ, and
likewise the cup of blessing is a partaking of the
blood of Christ. The body of Christ is given,
taken and eaten in the Supper only after an heavenly and spiritual manner. And the mean
whereby the body of Christ is received and
eaten in the Supper is faith."—Art. xxviii.
Faith, not in the mysterious efficacy of the bread
itself, or the wine itself; but in that of which
they are the emblems—faith in the body of our
Lord Jesus Christ as broken for us, in the blood
of our Lord Jesus Christ as shed for us: " Christ
in us the hope of glory"—" Made unto us salvation." So fed upon in faith, they are verily
and indeed received to the strengthening and refreshing of the soul, as our bodies, not our souls,
are strengthened and refreshed by the bread and
wine:—" by the faithful"—and by the faithful
only: the elements are of no more value than
they were before their consecration; they ac-

quire no inherent efficacy to do us good or harm: to them that receive them not worthily, they are what they always were, material elements that can affect the body only.

"This is my body which is broken for you." A great deal of conscientious scruple about the using of these words has arisen in the church at various times, and to all that has been written and said, we cannot expect to add weight on either side. Christ himself used them: and of course the inspired apostles used them, in neither case addressing a pure communion of accepted saints. The subject taken fully involves the whole disputed question of general and particular redemption, with the various shades of difference, which I am sure there are in men's opinions, between the two extremes.— To me it appears quite irreconcileable with the plain language of Scripture, to maintain that Christ did not, in some sense, die for the whole world; that he did not love the whole world when he died for it; or that he did not make a satisfaction and atonement sufficient for the sins of all mankind. Unless we could know what would have followed on the first transgression, had no redemption been designed, we cannot judge how much the world has gained by the suspension of its final sentence, by the long-suffering and forbearance, the time and opportunities, the ameliorations and restraints, and providential influences, which are all the purchase of redeeming love, and paid for by the sacrifice of Christ. We cannot estimate how much of Adam's forfeiture that prospective sacrifice at once brought back: but we know so much as this, that but for the atonement to be made for sin, God and man had then been eternally separated: and whatever passages of love and mercy have been between them since, are benefits derived from the atonement. In what sense Jesus died for the millions who never heard of him, and to what extent his death may have been beneficial to them, is indeed beyond our knowledge: but to say that he did not, in any sense, die for those who reject him, appears to me a contradiction in terms; because if he died only for the saved, no one can be guilty of rejecting him. I believe that Christ died for the sin of all mankind, in so far as sin is not actually their own, but derived to them from their first federal head— thus leaving them freed from the penalty of original sin, to answer only for their own transgressions: with how much light of natural conscience or superadded grace, we know not; but certainly enough to make them responsible for what they do. I believe, also, that by the death of Christ a way of reconciliation with the Father is opened, leave of approach is given, a means of communication is afforded, of which every man may avail himself if he will:— it has purchased for all of us the right to pray, the right to plead its value in our prayers, and ask the application of its benefits to our souls: it has opened the portals of heaven to let the petition pass, and disposed the Eternal One to be attent; how then, can we say he has not died for all? Nevertheless, I cannot consider this to be the meaning of the words made use of in the administration of the Sacrament; but rather that Christ meant, and the church acknowledges and every believer should understand a great deal more than this, when the words are addressed to 'a congregation of faithful men.' When Jesus said, " My body which is broken for you—my blood which is shed for many," I think he used the words in a sense in which they can only apply to those who are, what the first disciples were—what we in baptism profess to be, and by presenting ourselves at the table do pretend to be—members of Christ, children of God, and heirs of the kingdom of heaven: in scripture language, chosen in him before the foundation of the world—called to be saints— born again of the Holy Ghost—who walk not after the flesh, but after the Spirit. Addressed to the faithful recipient of the bread and wine, these gracious words do surely mean to say, not merely that Christ has died to afford us an opportunity of being saved, but that by his death he actually has saved us—that his body broken. has expiated our sins, that his blood shed has. secured eternal happiness for us, and that he not only proposes, but engages to preserve our bodies and souls to everlasting life. In the words of our own communion service, " when with a penitent heart and lively faith" we receive that holy sacrament, we do actually, not prospectively, " dwell in Christ and Christ in us: we are one with Christ and Christ with us:" manifestly a state of present, not of future or problematical salvation. The difficulty, therefore, returns upon us: how can these words be addressed to a mixed number, of whom the minister does not know this to be the case, nor has any strong ground for believing it: and who in fact do not believe it of themselves, nor so much as care to have it so in any serious manner. I can only repeat my opinion that we have the authority of Christ and the apostles for taking men upon their profession, and so pronouncing on them a benediction which is only valid if the profession be a true one. As it is said to the apostles in another case—" First say, peace be to this house—and if the Son of peace be there, your peace shall rest upon it: if not, it shall turn to you again."

" This do in remembrance of me." Blessed Jesus, could they forget thee? They had heard thy words, such as never man spake—they had seen thy works, such as no other man had done—thou hadst chosen them, and kept them and loved them, even as the Father loved thee. Could they forget thee, blessed Lord? Our

hearts sink within us while we read the words.
He has suffered for us, he has saved us, he
lives for us in heaven: He has given us all he
has—He has given us himself—our present
life and our eternal joy; and must we be reminded—must we have signs and emblems
to waken our memory and warm our hearts?
—He knew it: and He provided them—
He even requires of us this memorial of his
death, lest the world forget that he has visited
to save, and will return to reign.   But we do
not care about it—we do not understand it—
we are afraid to take it, and we will let it alone.
Lamb of God, whatever reason we have to be
afraid, we shall not find it in the memory of
thee!   There had been nothing seen of thee
but love—nothing heard or known of thee
but goodness—not one repulsive look to them
that sought thee—not one refusal to them that
asked thy help—not a word of discouragement
even to thy enemies, if they would turn to thee
again: they who rejected thee were repaid
with tears; and they who crucified thee only
with thy prayers.   And there has been no
change.   "As oft as ye eat this bread and
drink this cup, ye do show forth the Lord's
death till he come."   The lion of the tribe of
Judah is not in the feast—the judge, the aven-
ger is not there; but " in the midst of the throne
a Lamb as it had been slain"—touched with the

feeling of our. infirmities—waiting to be gracious—" Behold, I stand at the door and knock;
if any man hear my voice and open the door, I
will come into him, and will sup with him, and
he with me."

CHAPTER IV.

ON THE BENEFITS EXHIBITED AND RECEIVED IN THE LORD'S SUPPER.

"GREAT is the mystery of godliness! God manifest in the flesh!" With entire submission of the intellect to the ˉdictum of Scripture, with the simplicity of a little child, that comes not to argue with its teachers, but to learn; with the lowliness of one who is of yesterday and knows nothing, willing to become a fool that he may be wise, we approach, and invite others to approach this great incompassable mystery. If there be any of a higher mind, they need not follow us, for we cannot help them. Reason puts itself to silence at the outset, and thenceforward has no more to say; for it tells me that the less cannot comprehend the greater; that the finite cannot compass the infinite; that there is not, and never can be a work of God perfectly and entirely understood by human intellect. If it be said that God can reveal it to us: He does reveal to us what we could not discover of his doings, to the extent that our understandings can embrace. Or, He can give us understanding: He does give us understanding in a measure, and he increases the measure continually by impartation from himself; and perhaps will go on increasing it through all eternity; but it will be the understanding of the creature still, never commensurate with his own, and therefore, I conceive, never sufficient to the perfect comprehension of his works. In heaven we shall be spirits, but we shall not be gods. There are mysteries of God which angels do not know—and—itself a mystery at which we bow our heads in acquiescent wonder —there was a secret which the co-eqnal Son of God declared He did not know; because, as touching his manhood he was inferior to the Father, and took upon him, as I suppose, in the season of his humiliation, something of the limitation of finite being. Proud disputants! climb to the lofty summit of the mountains, and tell us what you see: cities, and plains, and rivers spreading wide, an expanse inconceivable to them upon the plain. And what beyond? Relate whence comes the river, and whither goes it. A barrier impenetrable bounds your vision, and other mountains intercept your view. Leave the earth then, and go with the aeronaut beyond the clouds; hundreds of miles lie now exposed before you, and nothing intervenes to bar your vision. Tell us what is doing in all that space, so curiously brought within your ken. The space is very wide and very wonderful, but your eyes can distinguish nothing; beyond a certain limit, it lies an unfeatured

mass, of which you can tell nothing but that
there it is.   Let us be ashamed for our assumption and insubmission.   God has raised us from
the midnight ignorance of our fallen nature, and
given us to see his holy purpose of redemption;
he has revealed to us the plan and method of
salvation, and given us to understand its progress, and foresee its blessed issue.   He has ex-
panded our finite vision beyond the beginning
or the end of time, back to the triune Jehovah's
covenant to redeem, and forward to the eternal
bliss of the redeemed.   But it is the creature's
eye that is brought to gaze upon the Creator's
discovered purpose—the bounded, limited capacity of a mortal man, that is to scan this revelation of the mysteries of God.   Well might we
stand at once confounded and amazed—silenced
and enraptured, abased and satisfied at once,
and with Job exclaim, " Mine eye hath seen
thee, behold I am vile."   Enough indeed has
been revealed to satisfy every feeling and occupy every faculty of our souls; straining the
longing eyes to catch a further glimpse as the
light of grace arises on the immensitude.   Natural reason sees nothing, absolutely nothing,
of wisdom, or love, or justice, in the vicarious
sufferings of Jesus Christ, to the Jews a stumb-
ling-block, and to the Greeks foolishness; too
improbable to be taken upon credit, and too
ureasonable to bear examination.   Sooner than
contend with an unbeliever on this ground, I

7

would admit the whole. God's plan of redemption for the recovery of the fallen world, is so improbable, that the wit of man could never have invented or conceived it; so unreasonable, that the creature who could, prior to its revelation, have expected or anticipated such an interposition on his own behalf, might have been thought insane. But if this most marvellous, most improbable and inconceivable device, has proved itself fitted to effect its purpose, I think the very fact should go to show that it is the offspring of a greater mind than his, who cannot appreciate it. I am sure we should conclude so in the little sphere of human capability, varying as it were a hair's breadth, one above another. We do not expect the infant of days, and the mean in capacity, to value the productions of the learned and the skilful. The mechanic who stands by and sees his machinery do the work that he was used to do with manual labor, thinks, if he thinks at all, how great beyond his own was the power that invented a machine of which he understands not the mechanism, still less the principle, but discovers the excellence in the results. In the plan of redemption, however the natural mind sees not even so much as this. Ignorant of the real nature of sin and its inseparableness from destruction, and ignorant of the perfection of deity which admits not that one attribute should exalt itself against another, that justice and truth

should concede to love and mercy, the sinner
sees neither danger nor difficulty in his position;
it requires only an extension of divine indulgence for the present infirmities of his nature, and
a grant of divine aid to enable him to overcome
them. He sees, in fact, no reason why the
Almighty creditor should contrive so expensive
and difficult a scheme for the payment of a debt,
which it was at his pleasure to remit. Even in
this depth of ignorance, it would become the
creature to put his hand upon his lips and say,
How can I judge the plans of the Omnipotent?
Let him declare to me what he has done, and I
shall know that therein is wisdom, because that
He is wise.

But this he does not. Such a declaration the
Deity has made, and man, in his profundity of
darkness, refuses to believe till he has judged it.
God will not suffer this. I am persuaded he
will in no instance suffer that a man's reason be
satisfied, before it is submitted to his authority.
Hence religion is ever made to begin with faith:
not sight, not knowledge, not understanding,
but belief. And thence I infer, that it is to depart from God's appointed mode of teaching, to
attempt to satisfy the intellect of the fitness and
wisdom of the atonement, before it is accepted
on the testimony of the written word. Convince
the gainsayer, if you can, that the Scripture is
the word of God: show him, if you can, the
plain annunciation of the atonement in it: he is

then at the point, at which he must believe the
testimony, without a question more: and from
that point forward, but never, as I apprehend,
before, will the wisdom of the divine purposes
be unfolded to him, and knowledge be added to
his faith, and the growing light of grace disclose
to him as much of the divine purpose of redemption, as his capacity, as a creature is capable of
apprehending. This process cannot be reversed.
You cannot first convince another, or convince
yourself, that the substitution of Christ was a
wise and necessary contrivance, and thence
descend to accept the revelation of it, because
you have found it worthy of his wisdom who
reveals it. " Except ye become as little children,
ye can in no wise enter into the kingdom of
God." Our progress in the kingdom of God is
unequal; different minds are led by different
paths, and our attainments, under divine grace,
are considerably affected by the natural bent and
character of the mind. Next to that simplicity
of heart, which is the gift of grace, clearness in
the understanding, and decision in the character,
are perhaps the greatest gifts to advance the
life of faith: but whatever varieties be found
within the kingdom, the entrance is but one, it is
the same to all. "As little children," whose
first lessons are of facts imparted, and received
as they are told, before they can be subjected to
the understanding, or verified by experience.
This done, the reason submitted to divine au-

thority, and the understanding enlightened by
the Holy Spirit, there is no faculty, no power
in man, that may not be brought to bear upon
the disclosures of revelation. Knowledge of
God, his wisdom and his ways, are a part of the
gift of salvation. Little indeed does the awakened spirit know, on its first reception of the
Gospel upon divine authority, what it will afterwards discern of the amazing wisdom, the overwhelming goodness that devised and carries out
this plan of redemption: little indeed foresee
how the enlarging intellect will revel in the expanse before it, to which there is always an hori-
zon, but never a termination—a limit to vision,
but none to expectation of what may be beyond;
and while all he reaches is wisdom, and all he
glances at is love, the advancing saint has little
mind to question or dispute against anything
not yet within his ken. If any of our readers be
otherwise minded, we can only ask them to go
back with us, and learn as we have learned,
the wisdom of the atonement in its efficiency to
save; the fitness of the remedy in the cure it has
effected; the loving-kindness of the gospel-scheme
in the extremity from which it has relieved in
us; in the hope, and peace, and joy it has given
in exchange for the desperation of our native
misery.

Poor leprous-stricken sinner! go, show thyself
to the priest, that he may certify thee if thou art
healed indeed; and if thou art, thou wilt be

7*

more disposed to lay thy reason, and all thou hast a sacrifice upon the altar, than to exercise it upon the justness and probability of the means that have been used to cure thee: if not, such speculations will never help thee. Thou must go back, and in the simplicity of a believing heart, in the attitude of a suppliant, not a disputant, exclaim, " O Lord, thou Son of David, have mercy upon me." The sentence will not wait thy approbation of it. " He that believeth in the Lord Jesus Christ, shall be saved; he that believeth not, shall be damned." " They eat and drink their own damnation, not discerning the Lord's body."

The Sacrament is an exhibition of the vicarious sufferings and death of Jesus Christ, and of the benefits derived from them, to those who, with a true faith and penitent heart, turn unto him, and by the power of his Spirit become incorporated with him, in that taking of the manhood into God, which constitutes the great truth of Christianity, the eternal mystery of revealed religion. In some sense it commemorates all that the Jewish sacrifices foreshowed: but as the manner of the atonement has now been fully manifested in the event itself, those bloody signs and figures that exhibited it, are no longer necessary; and it appears to me that the Christian ordinance, while it certifies the fact of the death of Christ, and keeps its verity in mind, more minutely exhibits the application of the atone-

ment to the soul, and the benefits received thereby. It exhibits Christ the sinner's substitute:
once dead and now alive for us; and we in him
once dead, and now alive for ever. Once indeed we were dead without him, "for in Adam
all died," dead souls and dying bodies, both fore-
doomed to an eternal existence, for its essential
misery called death. To reverse this half-exe-
cuted sentence, was the end of the atonement.
We may think it was very easy; God could have
forgiven the past, and remitted the remainder of
the penalty. I do not presume to say whether
he could or not: but I see that pardon comes too
late, when the sentence is already executed: man
was dead: "In the day that thou eatest, thou
shalt die." Severed from the source and suste-
tenance of life, cut off from that communication
of the deity, whence only good can be derived,
man lay like the trunk of an uprooted tree, which
keeps for a season the form and coloring of life,
and puts forth some feeble shoots, as if it were
alive. Mere pardon would avail little to the
soul already separate from God, and dead in
trespasses and sins, unless that which was done,
could be undone, and the past retrieved. But
could not God do this too? I cannot tell: but
mutability is an attribute of weakness: to do
and to undo, to say and unsay, is the creature's
shame. In a mere mortal, we require some
fresh light, or influence, or evidence to excuse a
change of mind. What light, what influence,

what subsequent discovery could act upon the
eternal mind, that he should unwill to-day, what
he willed yesterday, and bring to life his slain?
So much I see, though it is little enough, of
where the difficulty of man's recovery lay. As
a moral difficulty, we have an imperfect illustration of it in our case as parents; very imperfect, indeed, because our want of foresight has
part in our embarrassment. To deter our children from an act of disobedience, we threaten a
certain punishment, which, when the fault has
been committed, we are very unwilling to inflict: but our word must be inviolate, and our
authority maintained: against the pleasure of
all parties, the penalty must be enforced: a sort
of moral necessity from which the parent sometimes secretly relieves himself, by bringing in a
third person, to beg as a favor to himself, or for
some invented reason, that the culprit may escape the infliction: no parallel to the plan of
substitution, wherein the full penalty is inflicted:
but a faint illustration of the moral difficulty—
if we may at all apply that word to deity—how
God should be just, and yet the justifier of him
that had sinned.

We conceive further of the penalties of the
divine law, that unlike the sanctions of human
legislation they are not arbitrary appointments,
but necessary consequences, which it needs an
interference of power to prevent, but none to
inflict; misery follows sin: sin itself is misery;

and the soul that sinneth dies of course, without any measures taken to put that soul to death; though divine interference would be indispensable to prevent the consequences following the cause. Without all controversy, however, the fact was so; the living were dying and the dead were dead; animal life was wasting fast away, and spiritual life was already in its grave, buried in time and sense. In the great work of redemption, the one grave had to be opened and the other closed; earth, the soul's present grave, must be made to give up her dead; and hell, its eternal grave, must close her gates for ever. It was necessary that the substitute should be one who could not only receive upon himself our death, the death of the whole world, but could in return communicate to us his life. We know that to communicate life is the exclusive attribute of Deity.

I will not, because I cannot, search into the counsels of Jehovah, to judge of the eternal covenant in which this exigence was foreseen and provided for, and the work of redemption undertaken in the vicarious sufferings of the Son of God, accepted by the Father, and applied by the Holy Spirit. How it was, or why; or whether it had been better otherwise, or could have been otherwise effected, is not an inquiry for us. The very doubt is a trespass upon the rights of Deity: the all-wise, the omnipotent, the incomprehensible. We receive it on His

fit dwelling place for us; and, carrying the idea
of substitution out, it would avail us little that
Christ were holy and happy, and ascended up
to heaven in our stead. Human language is
but poor machinery for the conveyance of divine
ideas: but union, rather than substitution, is the
idea to be conveyed, and is the more scriptural
term; from adhering to the former notion, I think
it may in some minds have resulted, that they
consider personal sanctification, as well as meritorious righteousness, to be imputed, not imparted, to the sinner: that Christ, who is indeed unto
us wisdom, and righteousness, and sanctification,
and redemption, is so in the sense of substitution
rather than impartation, instead of us, rather
than in us. But if this were so, he must likewise be happy in our stead, and alive to God in
our stead, and well-pleasing to the Father in our
stead: which is at variance with the Scripture
declaration, that we are all this in him; not pu-
tatively, but really—"Accepted in the beloved."
"Alive in Christ." "Transformed by the renewing of your mind."

This union of the believer with Christ, with
all its blessed consequences, pervading as it
does the whole language of the Gospel, is com-
prehensively set forth by St. Paul in Rom. vi.
"As many of us as were baptized into Jesus
Christ, were baptized into his death. Therefore
are we buried with him." "Knowing this
that our old man is crucified with him."

"Likewise reckon yourselves to be dead indeed
unto sin, but alive unto God." And he argues
the necessity of this, inasmuch as without being
partakers of Christ in his death, we could not
be freed from the dominion of sin. "Our old
man was crucified with him, that the body of
sin might be destroyed: for he that is dead is
freed from sin." The believer, then, who
neither has died, nor ever is to die in his own
person for the expiation of his sins; who neither
has lived, nor ever will live so as to merit any
thing at the hands of God; who has not, and to
all eternity will not have wisdom or righteousness, or sanctification, or life, or knowledge, or
strength, or understanding, in and by himself;
has, by virtue of a mysterious union with the
Son of God, both died to sin and risen again to
righteousness; and deriving all by communication from him, "the life which he now lives in
the flesh, he lives by the faith of the Son of
God." "I am crucified with Christ; nevertheless I live; yet not I, but Christ liveth in me."
And this union is the unfolded mystery, the
mysterious blessedness, exhibited to us in the
sacrament of the Lord's Supper. Not the manner of it; that has not been, and perhaps could
not be subjected to mortal apprehension: there
probably are neither words nor ideas through
which an impression of it could be conveyed;
neither a capacity of understanding into which
it could be received. I perceive but one

8

parallel, and that is a mystery deeper and
more inscrutable that itself—the union of the
manhood and the godhead in our Lord, so
utterly and entirely beyond my conception.
In both cases, the fact has been revealed, and
must be received by faith, without understanding. Received by faith, but not as a metaphy-
sical problem, a dry and cold and abstract
statement of theoretical truth. Though we
have taken our view of the Gospel mystery
from this point, it is not so we can realize it,
and enjoy it, and live upon it; it is not so it
is exhibited in the sacramental elements: the
wisdom, the mercy, the fitness, the eternal
blessedness of the believer's union with the
Saviour, is to be studied, verified, and enjoyed,
as it is here exhibited, in the results, in its
application to the soul of the sinner.

Our communion purports to be received " In
remembrance of his meritorious cross and passion, whereby alone we obtain remission of our
sins, and are made partakers of the kingdom of
heaven." Union with Christ does at once pass
us, as we have seen, from death in Adam with
all its immediate and eternal consequences, to
life in Christ with all its present light and
everlasting glory. In other Scripture terms—
" Out of darkness into marvellous light"—
" When we were dead in sins, hath quickened
us together with Christ"—" Born again, not
of corruptible seed"—a change more especially

exhibited in the sacrament of baptism. For
the communicant who with a true penitent
heart and lively faith presents himself at the
Lord's table, this is assumed to have been done
—born anew of the Spirit unto repentance, and
by faith received into communion with the Son,
he is considered, and called upon to consider
himself dead indeed unto sin, but alive unto
righteousness through Christ: a child of God,
an heir of Christ, and an inheritor of the kingdom of heaven, But who that in faith, or even
in hope has taken this position, has not found
that he wants something more? He is still to
his own consciousness the same miserable sinner. Salvation, perfected as it is for him, is
not yet perfected in him; sin lives, though it
reigns no longer. Satan is his enemy, though
not his king: pardoned though he is, and justified though he stands from every charge, if left,
he would return to folly; if allowed, he would
slay himself again; if unsustained, the divine
life within him will expire, and he will neither
bring forth fruit meet for repentance, nor continue to walk by faith in remembrance of his
high calling. How blessed! at this point of our
condition, is the truth of the believer's union
with the Lord; how welcome the sacramental
elements, in which are exhibited the very sup-
port we need: exhibited under the figure of
food: for the maintenance of life, and increase
of strength, and growth in stature. "For then

we spiritually eat the flesh of Christ, and drink
his blood; then we dwell in Christ and Christ
in us: we are one with Christ and Christ with
us." One with Him in whom all fulness
dwells: what fear that we shall want or be
found wanting? with Him who having died
unto sin once, liveth unto God—what fear that
we shall be brought into bondage of the wicked
one? Who being raised from the dead, dieth
no more—what fear that we shall ever die
again? One with him who has the Spirit without measure, how should we then come short
of its sufficiency for all things? This blessed
union was in the Apostle's mind when he ex-
claimed, "For all things are yours, whether
Paul, or Apollos, or Cephas, or the world, or
life, or death, or things present, or things to
come; all are yours, and you are Christ's, and
Christ is God's."

Such I understand to be the truth brought to
remembrance in the Lord's Supper, and these
the benefits exhibited therein. Our church
affirms, that as well as signs of those benefits,
"they are means whereby we receive the same,
and a pledge to assure us thereof." (Cate-
chism.)

"Insomuch that to such as rightly, worthily,
and with faith receive the same, the bread
which we break is a partaking of the body of
Christ, and likewise the cup of blessing is a partaking of the blood of Christ." (Articles.)

CHAPTER V.

OF THOSE WHO REFUSE TO COME TO THE LORD'S TABLE.

It is a fact—one indeed, of which man has made an evil use, but nevertheless, a fact, that God does very seldom, if he does ever, in this world, work without an agency—without the intervention of some apparent means for effecting that which He designs. "He maketh the winds his ministers and his messengers a flame of fire." Some body or some thing executes his most sure decrees. He took time, He used a process when he made the world; and man was formed out of the material dust. Even that sentence which has passed on all men, which has become inseparable from our being, and essential to mortality—even death never takes place without a second cause. In the natural world every thing is effected by an established agency, doing its work with the unconscious monotony of a machine, and yet achieving the most discriminating acts of justice or mercy. The rolling surge has no preference between the body it ingulfs, and the one it casts alive upon the shore—the east wind does not choose whose harvest it will blight or spare;

8*

they are the undiscerning agents of a discerning
God. There is scarcely an act of providence,
however striking and impressive, in which a
second cause is not perceptibly made, use of. If
otherwise, it constitutes that act miraculous: and
even in these more immediate interpositions of
the Deity, means, though not ordinary ones, are
commonly employed: there came a strong wind
to raise the waters of Jordan, and a destroying
angel to slay the first-born of Egypt. Man in
his wisdom gainsays this arrangement. Unsanctified knowledge on the one hand, perceiving
that the thing is so—that deeper research can
discover a cause for every thing, with effects so
regularly following, determines that the world
can do without a God, and finds an over-ruling
providence superfluous. Pious ignorance, on
the other hand, takes offence at the research of
science—Why inquire after means at all? has
not God done all things as he pleases, and must
he work by rule as men do? We know not, I
'apprehend, which is the highest act of sovereignty—to work with means or without them—
it is a mere assumption that to look for second
causes is to impeach the sovereign power of
God. If we may judge of what it becomes the
Almighty to do, by what He does, the presumption will be contrariwise: assuredly He works
always for his own greatest glory; He does
nothing upon earth without agency; and He has
not told us that he does in heaven. In the work

of grace the fact is still the same—God uses instruments for a work exclusively his own. We
speak with reverence when we say the Holy
Spirit is the first great Agent—because, though
it is Scripture language, inasmuch as God is continually said to work by the Spirit, to give the
Spirit, &c., we must never forget that the Holy
Spirit himself is God, and therefore, cannot assume the character of a second cause. This first
great agent of redeeming grace does sometimes
work without the interposition of secondary
means. He probably so acted upon the minds
of them of old, in what we understand by inspi-
ration—immediate and direct communication to
the heart. He may so act when his holy influence blows where it listeth, and we hear. the
sound thereof, but cannot tell whence it cometh
or whither it goeth. But we know that this is
not generally the case: the reading of the Scripture, or some other book—the preaching of the
Gospel—the arguments and influence of pious
friends, some striking act of Providence, religious
ordinances, sickness, suffering or misfortune,
may almost always be remarked as the means
made use of to bring us to the knowledge of salvation, to mature our faith, and make us meet
for heaven; though all that is effectual in these
things, is from first to last, the work of God, by
the agency of the Holy Spirit.

How vain, then, is man, that he should neglect
or despise even the least probable means of spi-

ritual benefit. The most casual providence, the most inefficient preacher, the most imperfect service, provided the truth of God be exhibited in them, may be made the instrument of bringing divine life into the soul, or cherishing it there. We know not what healthful influences we throw away, when from some motive of earthly profit or convenience, we remove ourselves from the society of God's people, from the pure preaching of the Gospel, the use of ordinances, and opportunities of public worship.

In the communion of the body and blood of Christ we have a means of grace that stands on the highest ground. It is a divine appointment —a positive command; and yet, who has not passed the doors of a church at the moment when the congregation are pouring out, hundreds after hundreds, on the crowded pavement? The old, the sick—they do not look as if they would live to come again: the young, the gay— a long and perilous journey is before them: the rich—how hardly shall a rich man enter the kingdom of heaven: the poor—at least the poor have need of consolation! But they are all gone: it is too common a sight to wonder at: the service is ended. No, indeed it is not. The doors have been closed upon a few score suppliants, whose voices echo through the vacant space—some solitary ones here and there in the lately crowded pews, shivering in the sudden depopulation. What are they about? Nothing extraordinary—it happens every month—they are *staying for the Sacrament!* Eternal Being, is thine eye intent upon this place, and dost thou see nothing extraordinary in the scene? Are these the only ones of all that crowd, for whom thy blood was shed, thy body broken, thy feast provided, and thy welcome given? These all the sinners in danger of forgetting thee, or sufferers that stand in need of comfort, or dying ones exposed to condemnation! It is not yet the time when *thou* wilt command that they shut to the door, and exclude for ever those that are not ready: it is not thy doing that these hundreds, these *christian* hundreds turn their backs upon thy table! Suppose for a moment we could come with authority to the church-door—human authority—all would listen then —and require that no one should pass out till they had inscribed upon a tablet their reason for not staying to receive the holy communion at this appointed time. How would it read? Of the greater number, the reply would be, "We have no particular reason—we never thought of staying—we never stay the Sacrament." Without a reason, and without a thought, they neglect a divine command: refuse to partake of an ordinance ordained by Christ himself, and pronounced by their own church necessary to salvation. We might well inquire why they call themselves Christians, and come to worship in this place? They of old who would not eat of the Paschal

Lamb at the appointed times, were to be cut off
from the congregation of the people. Another
number, a considerable number would put it
thus—"We stay three times a-year—we never
neglect to stay at Christmas and other particular
seasons." This is indeed better, but so small an
appetite is scarcely a sign of health: we are not
thought to thrive when our food produces satiety
—it is not the hungry guest, nor yet the loving
one that seldomest returns to eat and drink with
us. We might ask of these, why at those particular seasons they accept the benefits they now
refuse. "We are engaged—we are in haste this
morning." But surely they forget: this is no
working-day, they will break other laws presently to be relieved of the wearisome hours
that remain. "We are not prepared, we are not
fit to stay." Poor sinners! Jesus has tenderest
pity for the tears that should have blotted that
sentence while you wrote it—a Saviour's eye
has watched your trembling hand while you
inscribed that sentence against yourself—He has
thought upon the anguish of his soul when he
too felt the weight of unforgiven sin—when
Satan and the powers of darkness had their hour
with him, as they have now with you. It is
most likely true!—you are not prepared, you
are not fit to stay! But do you indeed know it?
Do you feel that you are not his—that you have
no faith to feed upon his flesh, or penitence to
seek remission from his blood—that you do not

know if he has died for you, or if there is any
virtue in his death to save—that you have not
examined yourselves whether you repent you
of your former sins, stedfastly purposing to lead
a new life?—nay, it was not necessary to examine—a thought is sufficient; you know you do
not. It is most likely so—and you must go
away: we cannot tell you otherwise—for this
time you must go away: And may the Spirit
write upon your heart the sentence you have
given. Jesus is long-suffering and of great
goodness—he willeth not the death of a sinner,
but rather that he should turn to him and live:
this may not, through his mercy, be the last time
you will be invited to his table: that door which
has been closed behind you, may not be the one
which the unready will knock at eternally in
vain. But lest you abide contented with the
condition in which you know yourselves to be,
bear with a word of truth concerning it. It is
here, under your own hand, that you are unfit
for heaven—unprepared to die—unrepentant,
unbelieving, unforgiven—and of course condemned to everlasting death. There is a remedy, but you refuse it—an invitation, but you
will not accept it—a command, but you will not
obey it. "Look unto me and be ye saved."
"All things are ready—come unto the marriage:
but they made light of it, and went their ways;
one to his farm, another to his merchandise."

The crowd is dispersed, the street is silent,

they have gone their ways. We have not kept
the register, but the Great Searcher of hearts
has; and such is the fact, as it lies exposed before him, with respect to the greater number of
the dispersing congregation. If the eyes of those
indifferent ones could be opened, not a soul but
would shrink with terror from the sight which
they fear not to exhibit before the face of Him
who is of purer eyes than to behold iniquity.
" But the God of this world hath blinded the
minds of them that believe not, lest the light of
the glorious Gospel of Christ, who is the image
of God, should shine unto them."   " Their eyes
are closed that they cannot see, and their ears
are heavy that they cannot hear;" but whether
they will hear, or whether they will forbear,
whoever they be that wilfully refuse to come to
the Lord's Supper, this is the truth of their condition.   They are dying creatures: some will die
to-night and more to-morrow—many before
another sacrament, and all within four-score
years. They are sinful creatures, " who have
done what they ought not to have done, and
left undone what they ought to have done," till
there is no health in them by reason of their
sins; and of this sickness they may die eternally—consigned to sure and everlasting woe. This
is not a condition that may befal them some
time; it is what they are now: now that they
walk so confidently and carelessly away: dead
in one sense, and dying in another—dead souls

and dying bodies, murdered both by sin: let
them alone, and they are dead for ever! "If
our Gospel be hid, it is hid to them that are
lost." Sinners think of condemnation as something that is to be; and since to mortal vision
whatever is future is uncertain, they feed upon
this uncertainty and call it hope. Uncertain!
How then say the Scriptures—"Death passed
upon all' men, for that all have sinned." "By
one, judgment came upon all men unto condemnation." "In Adam all died." "He that believeth not is condemned already, because he
hath not believed in the name of the only-begotten Son of God." Man, as a sinner, is not in
the condition of an untried criminal, waiting,
between hope and fear, the time of trial, uncertain to be convicted or acquitted; that vague fallacious dream of many a lost one! Such a criminal may hope in spite of conscious guilt;
because his guilt may not appear; the evidence
may be insufficient, the judge may lean to cle-
mency, or the legal penalty may not attach. But
the sinner's guilt waits for no evidence, requires
no trial; every thought of his heart, every criminal movement of his soul has lain open from
all eternity to the Almighty judge; he will be
brought up for judgment, not for trial: nay, the
sentence is already past; "the soul that sinneth,
it shall die;" it is the execution only waits!
Woe to us, if even that be not past too: if the
substitute has not already died—if our sentence

9

has not been executed on another—if we were
not in Christ, when he was brought up from
prison and from judgment, nailed in him on the
cross, laid with him in the grave; woe to us, unless judgment and justice have done with us,
and " there remaineth no condemnation to them
that are in Christ Jesus." The uncertainty is
all our own, and ours will be the discovery at
the day of judgment. " Whosoever was not
found written in the book of life, was cast into
the lake of fire:"—The Lamb's book of life—
found written—not written then;—that is no
day of pardon or acquittal: we must be pardoned now, justified now, united now to Him, who
has made an end of sin, and put the sinner beyond the reach of judgment.

" Well, we hope we are, or that at least we
shall be before we die; it does not depend upon
going to the Sacrament." If a traveller has
taken a contrary road, he may hope, and we
may hope, that turning back he will attain his
end: but to hope that he will reach it by going
on, is the trust of folly; it is impossible! Salvation does not indeed depend on going to the
Sacrament—Judas went there, and Satan entered into him—but it does depend on our being
brought into that state of mind, in which
nothing but necessity could keep us from it.
We never argue that our children's love does
not depend upon their obedience, their compliance with our wishes, and enjoyment of our

presence; or say that our health does not depend upon our appetite, or strength, or ease; that the sanity of our mind does not depend on the rationality of our actions and conclusions; because in natural things we make no confusion between the evidence, and the cause of our condition. Coming to this table is not the cause of our faith and repentance, any more than faith and repentance are themselves the cause of our salvation: but as faith and repentance are necessary to salvation, the sacraments are necessary as evidences of these, and by inference, as our church declares them, necessary to salvation: as acts of obedience to the divine command, they are indispensably necessary to our abiding in his love. "If any man love me, he will keep my commandments." "This do in remembrance of me."

All who wilfully and without a sufficient reason refuse to come to the Lord's table, do in the very act of departing from the church in which it is celebrated, make a public declaration of one of these things;—either that they do not value the benefits to be received thereby, or that they are not entitled to partake of them. Comparing either position with the language of Scripture, most fearful is the judgment we give against ourselves. Suppose that we do not value these benefits, that is, we do not believe them to be of any value. It is an awful predicament, when we consider what it is we dis-

believe, and the authority we set at nought in
doing so. "This is my body which was broken for you." "This is my blood of the New
Testament, which was shed for many, for the
remission of sins." "As often as ye eat this
bread, and drink this cup, ye do show forth the
Lord's death till he come." "The body and
blood of Christ, which are verily and indeed
taken and received by the faithful in the Lord's
Supper." "The strengthening and refreshing
of our souls by the body and blood of Christ, as
our bodies are by the bread and wine." "The
benefit is great, if with a truly penitent heart
and lively faith, we receive that holy Sacrament; for then we spiritually eat the flesh of
Christ, and drink his blood, then we dwell in
Christ, and Christ in us; we are one with
Christ, and Christ with us."

The testimony of God and of the church are
one: if we receive neither, why have we come
to church at all? "Into whose name then were
ye baptized?" Why have we offered so many
prayers in Jesus' name, pleaded so many times
this blood which we do not value, this body
broken, which we do not care for; and given
so many thanks for benefits in which we do not
believe? What sudden fear has seized us, of
becoming hypocrites if we stay any longer in
the church this morning? We have been
breathing hypocrisy ever since we entered it.
You deny this: you are shocked at the suppo-

sition that you do not believe in the benefits of
Christ's death and passion; it is of course that
we believe it; so much of course, that we do
not require the sacramental pledges to assure us
thereof. Are you so sure of God's mercy, that
you need not seek it in the way of his appoint-
ing: so sure of his love, that you need not do
the things that he has said? so sure of your
food, you need not eat it; of your medicine,
you need not take it? so penitent you need no
pardon; so faithful you need no grace; so grateful you need make no acknowledgements?
"God knows our hearts." Yes, he does know;
and whether you will come, or whether you
will not come, He has no discoveries to make—
He knows it all. But he who has nothing to
discover, has determined that nothing shall be
taken for granted: he will have no things of
course; he will have outward manifestation of
every inward feeling. "With the heart man
believeth unto righteousness, and with the
mouth confession is made unto salvation."
"Unless ye eat my flesh, and drink my blood,
ye have no part in me." God accepts no penitence without confession, no love without obedience, no grace without prayer, no faith without
profession. And what he does not accept, He
has not promised. He has not promised pardon, hope, or safety, apart from the means
appointed to convey them, to which end he
has especially ordained these holy mysteries.

9*

When we need not the blessings, we may dispense with the instruments. When faith is swallowed up in sight, and hope in joy, and death in victory; then the water courses will be cut off, and the waters called back to the fountain; and these holy sacraments will cease for us: "I saw no temple therein, for the Lord God Almighty and the Lamb are the temple of it." Rev. xxi. 22.

But, until the fulness of that time be come, to all who think they have no need of these, who refuse to come to the stream, that they may drink; to the tables, that they may be fed; who will not wash in Jordan, that they may be clean; who take all for granted—Christians of course—we may use the Apostle's words, "Because thou sayest I am rich, and increased with goods, and have need of nothing; and knowest not that thou art wretched, and miserable, and poor, and blind, and naked; I counsel thee to buy of me gold tried in the fire, that thou mayest be rich, and white raiment that thou mayest be clothed, and that the shame of thy nakedness may not appear; and anoint thine eyes with eye-salve that thou mayest see."

On the single alternative we have said something, but not enough; suppose you are not entitled to the benefits exhibited and received in the Lord's Supper, can you believe it and go in peace? If it is so, you have no part in Christ; no participation in his blood; no

benefit of his death; no remission of sin; no
sanctifying spirit; no help in life, no hope in
death, no promise for eternity: for these are
the benefits distributed to the faithful in the
Lord's Supper, to which you are not entitled.
And as there is no other name given under heaven whereby we may be saved, but the name of
Jesus Christ; in whose body and blood you cannot be partakers, there is but one sequence—you
are lost for ever! It is an awful sentence: but
it is yours, not ours; and the everlasting seal is
not yet affixed to it. The Saviour still repeats
the loving words, "Come unto me, all that travail and are heavy laden, and I will refresh
you." The scripture still contains this precious
truth, " God so loved the world that he gave his
only-begotten Son, to the end, that all that believe in him should not perish, but have everlasting life." " This is a true saying and worthy of all men to be received, that Christ Jesus
came into the world to save sinners." The
church repeats her slighted invitation, "Ye that
do truly and earnestly repent you of your sins,
and are in love and charity with your neighbor,
and intend to lead a new life, following the commandments of God, and walking henceforth in
his holy ways; draw near with faith, and take
this holy sacrament to your comfort." There is
yet time. " To-day," while there remaineth a
day, "if ye will hear his voice, harden not
your hearts." To-day, while it is called to-

day, lest any of you be hardened through the deceitfulness of sin." There is a day of grace, but no to-morrow. "For behold the night cometh in which no man can work." "There remaineth no more sacrifice for sin, but a certain fearful looking-for of judgment."

CHAPTER VI.

OF THOSE THAT ARE AFRAID TO COME.

WE have supposed a case—we have seen in
idea the recusant crowd disperse; and if the
master of the feast has said on the one hand,
"They that were bidden were not worthy,"
has he not cause to say on the other, "Were
there not ten cleansed? where then are the
nine? There is not found to give glory to God,
save this stranger." Jesus has watched the re-
ceding steps of some to whom nothing we have
said is applicable; who do indeed write the
same hard sentence against themselves; "they
are not fit, they are not ready now," and go
away in sorrow, not in scorn; intending to
return some better day. And we can fancy that
we hear the benignant voice again, as it spake
once to the disciples in the wilderness: "They
need not go away, give ye them to eat." The
divine master's feasts are all alike: "They have
fasted all the day and eaten nothing: if I should
send them away fasting, they will faint by the
way." Hunger was the preparation for that
miraculous feast. "Fetch hither the poor, and
the maimed, and the halt, and the blind." Others
had the invitation, but it was the hungry and

necessitous that had the feast. "Blessed are
they that hunger and thirst after righteousness,
for they shall be filled." The living water, the
life-giving bread, the manna that came down
from heaven, the wine and milk without money,
and without price, all his provisions are bestowed alike. "He filleth the hungry with good
things, and the rich he sends empty away."

Our title to partake of the Sacrament is the
same as our title to partake of Christ; we do not
purchase the tokens, while we take the grace for
nought; merit the shadows, and have the substance free. If the fears of the timid are to be
removed, I think they must be met upon this
ground: for whatever be the exclusive character of the ceremony, as limited to the family of
God, the seal of adoption is an invisible one;
until it be realised, sometimes slowly, often imperfectly, and it may be never fully, in the signs
of divine life within the soul. Admitting that
the benefits to be derived from the Holy Communion are confined to those who are alive in
Christ, and united to him by a living faith, and
cannot in any wise be partaken of by those who
are yet dead in trespasses and sins, which I
most fully do: I for myself must say, that I cannot agree with those who require that the communicant should certainly *know* that he is born
again of the Spirit, and made one with Christ,
before he presents himself to eat and drink at
the table of the faithful. It is one thing to be

in a state of grace, and another to realise confidently the fact that we are so. I doubt if the apostles themselves, at the time they received their first commnnion, could have met the inquiry so put; though to the simple question, " Lovest thou me?" they could all have answered, " Yea, Lord." Many are renewed in the Spirit, and justly hope they are, and with more or less confidence, do even believe they are—who would yet hesitate to approach the altar, and declare that they know themselves to be so. The suggestions of Satan, and the infirmities of the flesh, produce uncertainties, where there need be none; while there is many a living member of the body of Christ, in whom the signs of life are for a season so indefinite, and overborne by earthliness, it is only God can know if they be genuine: the doubting disciple may be afraid, and may have some reason to be afraid that sin has still dominion over him: 'but so far from forbidding such a one, awakened to a sense of his condition, and seeking deliverance by the blood of Christ, I should invite and urge him to communicate, as a means through which more grace might prayerfully and hopefully be expected.

Satan is very subtle, and there is a principle within us more subtle even than he; the principle of self-righteousness, so tenacious, it will catch at the shadow of a straw to maintain itself. Christ is our title to salvation, but where

is our title to Christ? Here are the emblems of
his blood shed, and body broken, but how do
we know if they are designed for us? The
secret decrees of the eternal godhead have not
been found too distant a place to hide away the
sinner's title to his Saviour, lest haply he should
find it, and take possession. How do we know
if we were in Christ before the foundation of the
world, chosen of God and precious, foreknown
and predestinate to life and union with him;—
without which we cannot eat his flesh, or drink
his blood, or appropriate the blessings of these
holy mysteries? I believe that Jehovah has,
because he says he has, his hidden ones, his
secret covenant, his eternal purpose, his fixed
immutable decrees. But, like the plan itself of
their salvation, the election of grace is the secret
of omnipotence, into which we are not called
upon to look, nor can look, except as it is manifested in its effects. We are not called upon to
know, we cannot know, that we were in Christ
when he died, or in the covenant when he undertook to die, otherwise than by discerning that
we are in him now. "Say not in thine heart,
Who shall ascend into heaven?—that is to bring
Christ down from above; or Who shall descend
into the deep?—that is to bring Christ again
from the dead. But what saith it? The word
is nigh thee, even in thy mouth, and in thy
heart: that is the word of faith which we
preach." Whatever may have been done, or

written, or determined in the eternal councils of
Jehovah, all that we are cognizant of is trans-
acted here: salvation was wrought out on earth,
within the reach of mortal sense and knowledge:
and it is on earth that our title to it must be
made out, our interest in it made sure, not by
discovery of our names written in those uno-
pened books of heaven, but in the traces of the
Spirit working in our hearts, in the word that
our mouths can utter, and the faith that our
hearts can feel; the word of promise that tells
us, such and such are the heirs of salvation; in
the answer of faith that testifies we are such and
such, and takes the promise home. The doctrine of an elect and foreordained people, in con-
nection with the responsibility of man, is a mystery as unsearchable to human reason, as that of
the atonement, God manifest in the flesh: but
like that also, it appears to me in its application
to the soul, the simplest thing possible: never
more simply exhibited, than in the teaching of
Him, to whom those secret decrees were no
secret, but who used them only as he left them
for our use. When Jesus had his pre-elected
twelve to bring out from that unbelieving nation,
his first address to them was, "Follow me;" the
same it is to all of us, as if they were to do it of
their own free-will. "If any man will be my
disciple, let him forsake all that he hath, and
follow me, and he shall have treasure in heaven;"
as if it were submitted to their preference. "If

10

any man will keep my commandments, the Father will love him ;" as if divine love were the reward of obedience. "Thy faith hath saved thee;" as if faith were the originating cause of salvation. "Ask, and ye shall have, seek and ye shall find, knock and it shall be opened unto you;" as if the first movement was to be their own, something which they could do if they would, and were responsible if they would not. Would he have satisfied them, think ye, if they had wanted first to be assured of their interest in him who bade them follow; if Peter had refused to leave his nets, and Matthew his receipt of custom, till they could make out their title in the eternal covenant: if they had insisted on realising the personal application, the individual benefit of that bread before they ate it, that wine before they drank it:—"What is that to thee?" Jesus addressed all upon their responsibility: with motives and inducements that should act upon their determination: but Jesus did not leave them without the blessed assurance of their title to salvation; nor in any mistake as to the means by which it had become theirs: for he tells them they were the Father's, before they became his, that he had chosen them, they had not chosen him; and blessed were they whose names were written in heaven. This is irreconcileable. It is so: and be it so. But here are the precious emblems of the body and blood of Christ; they are offered, not to a person, but to a character, invited not by name, but by description. What wait ye for—"Come to the supper."

We wait to be assured that we answer the description by which we are invited. And so indeed we must, "Ye that mind to come to the holy communion of the body and blood of our Saviour Christ," must "consider how St. Paul exhorteth all men to try and examine themselves before they presume to eat of that bread and drink of that cup." There is an unpreparedness that with a bold and confident step comes often to the table, mindless enough of the searching eye that marks the ill-dressed guest, and only spares to cast him out, because there is yet a time to discover his own nakedness. Pride, impenitence, and unbelief are spots in the feast of charity that Jesus sees; guilty now, as they were heretofore, of his most precious blood; now of despising, as before of shedding it. Jesus sees many now, as heretofore he saw but one, who having eaten of his bread, will lift up his heel against him; will presently be found among his enemies; profaning his Sabbaths, disputing his word, denying him for gain, or forsaking him for pleasure. But these are not they whom fear withholds, or a sense of unworthiness keeps back.

At this thy table, blessed Lord, thou hast indeed fulfilled thine own injunctions—thou has not bidden the rich that can give to thee again; thou hast called the poor, who can make thee no recompense, until thy redeemed shall be themselves thy recompense—the joy that is set before thee. And thy bread and wine are like thy own precious blood; not intended for the righteous, nor for the just made perfect; they are for sinners—for repenting sinners as such, who are not worthy so much as to gather up the crumbs under thy table; whose sins are grievous; whose burden is intolerable. Are any such afraid to come? Then I can only say, I find no other name or title, or description, under which they are invited. I cannot find it written, Come, ye washed, ye cleansed, ye perfect ones; come hither, ye strong, ye sanctified, ye assured. It is " Come unto me, all ye that are weary and heavy-laden, and I will refresh you." " Let him that is athirst come, and whosoever will, let him take the water of life freely." Willingness and need.—" The lost," it was the name of them that Jesus came to save: " Ready to perish"—it is the only readiness that Jesus speaks of. Our misery was the Saviour's inducement when he died, and our salvation his only desired reward. Sense of the one, and consent to the other, a truly penitent heart and living faith, are all the title now that he acknowledges. When the spirit is willing, but the flesh is weak; when the spirit is not willing, but is longing to be made so; when the heart is broken and can find no peace; nay, when the heart is stout, but desires to be broken, we would repeat our words—"Come ye to the supper."

But Satan has more to say—and he can quote Scripture too. There was one called and came, but he had not on a wedding garment. To keep the awakened soul from Christ as well as from his table, some notion of preparation is infused:—we must be better first, or more sure at least of our sincerity. We must dress ourselves before we go; we cannot go as we are into the kingly presence. Oh! it was no kingly presence-chamber when on that night in which He was betrayed, the man of sorrows sat among his few, and distributed the precious emblems without a word of sovereignty but this, " Take, eat." It was then that he girded himself to wash their feet; it was then he looked for some to take pity and there was none, and for comforters and found none. If there be a moment above every other in which perfect love should cast out fear, it would seem to be in approaching the sacramental table, where every terror of the Godhead is veiled under images of suffering, lowliness and grief. When I have looked upon the table spread, and tried to concentrate my thoughts upon the scene of that first supper, to realise the words as Jesus spake them, " Take, eat, this is my body which was broken for you," as they thrilled upon my soul, I have thought that pride and unbelief were the

10*

only unfitness for such a presence; there could not be a sinner willing and not welcome.

"Go into the highways and hedges, and as many as ye find, bid them to the feast. Men are not found on the highways in wedding dresses; the garment was provided for them at the feast; but he who was found without one had neglected to put it on: a beautiful illustration of the kingdom of God, where all that is required of us is provided for us. "Bring the best robe and put it on him." "Put ye on the Lord Jesus Christ." "That ye put on the new man, which after God is created in righteousness and true holiness." St. Paul's reproof to the Corinthians, is not that they came to the feast when they should have remained away; but that coming they had not received it in a proper manner, in a right state of mind, and with a due appreciation of its design:—"not discerning the Lord's body." It is not said, "Because many are weak and sickly among you, and many sleep, therefore ye are unfit partakers of this sacrament," as if weakness, and sickness, and torpor, were reasons for abstaining from the spiritual sustenance appointed for their relief. These unhealthy symptoms are said to be the consequences, not the cause, of the unworthy receiving of the sacred elements. When they ate the bread and drank the wine, their souls fed not upon Christ, they did not spiritually eat his flesh and drink his blood;

they did not discern, or realise, or perhaps
believe, the benefits to be received therein; they
profaned the rite by their levity, and denied it
by their unbelief, and were guilty of despising
both it and him. "For this cause many are
weak and sickly among you, and many sleep."
Because here is food and ye do not eat it: because here is medicine and ye do not take it;
because here are words of peace and love that
might waken the slumbers of the very dead,
and ye do not hear them;—what wonder if ye
both faint and sleep to death, and make yourselves guilty of your own destruction. But
where in all the Scripture is it written, "Ye are
too sick for my medicine; too faint for my food;
too weary and jaded for my voice to strengthen
you?" Certainly not in this passage, in which
the penitent sinner thinks he finds his prohibi-
tion, and the timid Christian reads the warning
that keeps him at a distance. "Let a man
examine himself," and so let him turn his back
upon my table; let him go sick, and weak, and
torpid to his home, and come again when he is
better! I have read this in other books; I
almost think I have heard it from the pulpit,
but I never could find it in the word of God.
Neither do I think the formulary of our church
places any such difficulty in the way of the
awakened but unestablished Christian; repentance for sins past, and faith in the atoning
sacrifice of Christ, and purpose to lead a holy

and religious life, are expressed without reference to our attainment in them—whether it be
the grain of mustard seed, or the fulness of the
stature of Jesus Christ, "We are not worthy
to gather up the crumbs under thy table."
" Trusting. in thy manifold and great mercies."
Now the very fear of the timid Christian implies a sense of unworthiness and conscious sin;
and his desire to come implies at least some
measure of belief in the efficacy of the blood of
Jesus, in which he seeks an interest, and in the
influences of the Spirit, of which he uses the
means.

The very coming in this mind is an act of
obedience, and such a one as was never rejected by Jesus upon earth. " Lord, if thou wilt,
thou canst make me whole," was no unaccepted
prayer. "Grant us, gracious Lord, so to eat the
flesh of thy dear Son Jesus Christ, and to drink
his blood, that our sinful bodies may be made
clean by his body, and our souls washed in his
most precious blood, and that we may evermore
dwell in him, and he in us." We confess our
misery and need: we profess our belief in the
power of the atoning, purifying blood; but all
that might present a difficulty to the weak believer in respect of his own attainments, is put
in the form of supplication. In no part of the
service are we called upon to say that we have
walked in all the commandments of the Lord,
or to promise that we will. Not one trembling

sinner, not one humble self-condemning saint,
would venture to draw near on such a bidding:
I could almost say, not one would be found at
the altar who had a right to come there; because the more sanctified the soul becomes, the
more does it perceive of its own defectibility;
and as the first step of faith is shame and self-
abhorrence, so every subsequent step is shame
and self-abhorrence still. Alas! the saint who
knows himself, best knows he has no more to
promise than he has to give. He comes not to
give an undertaking for himself—"Have patience with me and I will pay thee all;" forgive
the past, and I will serve and please thee for the
time to come. He comes to say, "Grant that
we may hereafter serve and please thee in newness of life, to the honor and glory of thy name."
The stedfast purpose, the honest desire, and the
believing prayer, are indispensable characters of
a living faith: but to wait till they are to our
own consciousness fulfilled, is to refuse the feast
till we can bring the provision with us. I have
not noticed the condition added by the church,
to be in love and charity with all men; because
I think no awakened soul can be long debarred
the communion on account of it; the Scripture
direction is plain, that if a man recollect that
his brother hath aught against him, he is not to
withdraw his gift and stay away, but to be immediately reconciled—to put away the resentment or the provocation, whichever be on his

side, and come again. "Let not the sun go
down upon thy wrath."

The new-born spirit thus faltering at the
threshold of the temple, does not know what
he will know as he proceeds—that the mountain which now seems to bar his approach to
God will continually present itself at every period of the life of faith: and he must do to the
last, what he might do at the first, say to it—
" Be thou removed and cast into the sea"—for
this power was not promised to the strength and
growth of faith, but to its smallest possible existence. That mountain mass of sin, which the
dawn of spiritual light so mistily discloses, will
not diminish as the day-light grows—clearer,
and blacker and more distinguishable each dark
feature lies, and the advancing saint could only
think that he grows worse, should he stand still
to gaze upon himself, instead of looking to
Jesus, the author and finisher of his faith. Let
the willing, but fearing communicant examine
himself—not upon his measure of faith or progress in holiness—he will come to no assurance
thus: let him examine himself what it is that
keeps his soul from Christ and from the blessings of this holy table: for I must ever treat the
two as one: he who knows that he has come
to Christ, cannot have a doubt that he is welcome here. The hesitation very probably ori-
ginates in believing a part instead of the whole
of the Gospel promise. We believe sometimes

that Christ has opened the gates of heaven for us, end left us to find the way to it as we can; has purchased for us the opportunity of salvation, and left it to ourselves to make effectual use of it; whence our uneasiness lest we mistake the way: Or having found, as we believe, the entrance gate, uncertain of strength and grace to persevere, we enter trembling and go on in fear. Or it may be that we accept from Christ the pardon of our sins, but look to ourselves for power to overcome them; justified in him, but sanctified in ourselves: like kingly grants of earth, to conquer and maintain the kingdom conferred upon us freely. Such thoughts as these lurk often in an unexamined faith, little suspicious of its own unsoundness, while mournfully desponding at its want of strength. If the willing candidate finds any thing of this sort in his mind, let him come and bring it with him to the altar—and see if it will stand before these pledges of the Saviour's love—if it is possible such a love has done but half its work. Gaze on the emblems of his body and blood, and hear his own words repeated, and think if it is possible that coming to him you should be refused—that trusting him you should perish. Contemplate that blood, and see if there can be anything for you to add to its sufficiency—consider that body, and see if anything can be wanting to finish the work he has begun: Has it been shed for an experiment—broken for a may be? "Draw near in faith, and take this holy Sacrament to your comfort." "They that were bidden shall not taste of my supper." Why? because they presumed upon an invitation not intended for them? No—but because when I had bidden them they were not willing. He that is not chosen is cast out; because he comes unbidden? No—but because when he comes he does not put on the robe of righteousness prepared for him, and wash himself in the fountain opened for sin and for uncleanness: he prefers his own tattered and polluted raiment, his cherished sins or virtuous pretensions, to the imputation of Christ's righteousness, and the imparted graces of the Holy Spirit.

CHAPTER VII.

OF THOSE THAT COME UNWORTHILY.

"MANY are called—but few are chosen." It
is the will of God, for the vindication doubtless
of his own truth and honor, that the doctrine
the most offensive to the natural heart, and the
most proudly resisted by the world, is that which
it is most continually destined both to witness
and to verify: the worshippers of Christ are the
few and not the many. Wherever the cross is
exhibited, it is the few and not the many, that
with a broken and a contrite heart bow down
before it; wherever, and however the Gospel
invitation is proclaimed, it is the few and not
the many that with a true and living faith accept
the promises and enter into rest. "For strait is
the gate and narrow is the way that leadeth
unto life, and few there be that find it." Few
was the church of God when it floated over the
waters of a drowning world; fewest of any people when he fetched it out of Egypt to be a
separated nation to himself—and fewer still
when all but three fell down before the golden
image Nebuchadnezzar the king set up. Few
were they when the Messiah came unto his
own, and his own received him not: when Jesus

11

with all his miracles, his power, his wisdom and his goodness, could gain but some hundreds to his side, and administered his first sacrament to only twelve. And since the Holy Ghost the Comforter has come, with all the out-pouring of his gracious Spirit, the spreading of his word and increase of his grace—what are we to say? Churches are opened, and the many of our population stay at home—the Holy Sacrament is administered, and the many of our Christian congregations go away.

And yet—even yet—" The kingdom of heaven is like unto a net that was cast into the sea and gathered of every kind." Few, as from the multitudinous ocean of this sinful world, the Gospel net draws in—small as the Christian Church is amid the shoals of scepticism and idolatry—the awful fact is so—it is God's abiding pleasure that it should be so—they are not all Israel that are of Israel—the bad fish are in the net—the tares are in the field—the goats are in the fold—there is a Judas seated at the table. God's time of final separation is not come— "Let them grow together until the harvest." He who from all eternity has known his own, has named but one test by which to try and prove them—" Believest thou in me;" often a secret between the soul and God; nay, sometimes God's alone, for He knows many a child whose stricken spirit does not know itself. Men would not have it so—men are wiser, and would discriminate; they would go in at once and rout them out: and hoping to exclude all but the elect of God, they make tests that God has never made, by which to try and know them. Subscribe these doctrines, join this particular church; we must know, and you must know that you are chosen of God, before we admit you to the communion of his saints. Yet when all is done, and we, poor leaders of the blind, are satisfied, your profession may be false, we may be mistaken, and you be lost ones.

I cannot express too strongly what I think of the wisdom of our church, in the very point on which it has been impugned; the freeness of her administration. The wisdom, I repeat, with which she addresses herself to all who shall be religiously and devoutly disposed, that do mind to come to the holy communion of the body and blood of our Saviour Christ; reminds them of the dignity of that holy mystery, and the great peril of the unworthy receiving of it; warns the impenitent and unbelieving not to come; and then addressing the communicants by such a description as can alone entitle them to draw near—"Ye that do truly and earnestly repent you of your sins," &c. leaves to themselves the peril of a false profession. A false profession it most truly is, if any one who ought to have been excluded, can proceed with the appointed words; if, not repenting, not believing, not purposing or wishing to amend, the bold, unfit com-

municant ventures to draw near upon such a
bidding, and pronounce the words appointed for
his use.

"If we would judge ourselves, we should not
be judged." You then who are coming and do
constantly or occasionally come to the table of
the Lord, consider well what the profession is
you are required to make: consider, that when
you have made it, and the church has accepted
it, and God has heard it, it may be a false profession. "And when the king came in to see
the guests, he saw there a man that had not on
a wedding garment." The Master did not
blame his servants for the incautious admission
of his unworthy guest, for he had bidden them
to gather together all that could be found, as
many as would, and bring them to the feast;
the graceless intruder bore the condemnation.
"Bind him hand and foot and take him away,
and cast him into outer darkness; there shall be
weeping and gnashing of teeth; for many are
called, but few are chosen." "After he had
received the sop,.Satan entered into him." The
moment when the superstitious, self-righteous
or impenitent soul has satisfied and dulled itself
by the performance of a religious duty, may not
perhaps be the time at which the forbearing and
most pitiful God will give the word of final
separation; but it is the very opportunity for
Satan to take more full possession of his own,
and harden the heart in unbelief and sin.   And

if he was present, as we see he was, at that most
holy feast, where Jesus and the chosen twelve
sat down alone, can we select a company so
pure, or shut the door so close, or leave so few
within, that he will not be one?

The benefit of the communion is limited to a
number—to the faithful. It is said to be received in taking the elements, not derived from
them; and limited to the condition of the recipient. " The benefit is great, if with a truly penitent heart and lively faith we receive the holy
sacrament: for then we spiritually eat the flesh
of Christ and drink his blood; then we dwell in
Christ, and Christ in us; we are one with Christ
and Christ with us." The church does not,
I apprehend, mean to say that the act of eating and drinking the elements, either occasions
us or entitles us to dwell in Christ; neither
makes us to be, nor proves us to be one with
him. The worthy or unworthy partaking of
them is an evidence, but not a cause of those
different states of mind to one of which the benefits are limited. This cannot, I think, be better
illustrated than in the material symbols through
which it is exhibited. God has chosen the foolish
things of this world to confound the wise, and the
commonest things of this world to illustrate the
most mysterious. Meat and drink are the most
frequent emblems of the divine operations within
the soul, " My body is meat indeed, my blood
is drink indeed." " Whoso shall drink of the

11*

water that I shall give him, shall never thirst; but the water that I shall give him, shall be in him a well of water springing up into everlasting life." Now we know that the bread and the wine, and the water, are useless indeed to one who is not alive; they cannot give life, nor restore it when extinct. So in the communion, if there be no living faith within, the soul cannot feed upon the body or blood of Christ, however it be exhibited before us, and shown forth by us. Sufficient it is, and good it is, but not available to us, until we be made alive by regeneration of the Holy Spirit. We know also that the corporeal food, the bread, the water, and the wine, cannot nourish the living frame unless they be taken into it: the contemplation of them will not feed us, nor the welcome to them, nor the mere persuasion that they are good for food. In like manner cannot our souls be benefited, whether by the sign or the thing signified, by the means of grace, or the pledge to assure us thereof, unless Christ be spiritually fed upon by faith in the receiving of the same. Regardless of the church's warning, and the great peril they incur, many there are, who come to the Lord's communion;—"They sit as my people sitteth;" who neither expect nor desire any such blessings.— They cherish no memory of Jesus' death; they seek no pledges of his truth and love; they want no comfort of his Spirit; they are not hungry that they should eat, nor thirsty that they should

drink, nor faint that they should be refreshed;
neither do they indeed anticipate any such occur-
rence from the administration of the supper.
They come on other business. They come to
satisfy the law of God by an act of devotion; to
satisfy their conscience by a profession of Christianity; they come to avoid some guilt or danger
that might attend upon absenting themselves, or
to derive some mysterious benefit from the performance; perhaps to get remission for past impenitence, forgetfulness, and unbelief, and ease
of mind in the continuance of them: or help to
establish their own righteousness, and grace to
procure salvation for themselves. They come
to the sacrament to be saved: not to remember
Him by whom alone is salvation. It is needless
to say they lose their errand, for at this supper
no such provision is prepared, and no such benefits are promised.

It would be difficult to say which are the
most unfit communicants, or which at Christ's
table the most unwelcome; they who bring
their virtues, or they who bring their sins—they
who do not intend to renounce their righteous
pretensions, or they who do not intend to renounce their unrighteous practices; the one coming dressed in tissues of their own weaving, the
others in all the vileness of their native rags;
both equally refusing to put on the garment of
salvation Christ has provided for them. The
two descriptions would probably comprehend

the unfit communicants in general—defect of
principle on the one hand, and of its practical
influence on the other: if indeed they be ever
separated. We much doubt it, although we
consider them under the different aspects unbelief assumes. It was asked of old, " Ye who desire to be under the law, do ye not hear the
law?" and it was said by the same authority—
" Woe unto you scribes and Pharisees, ye make
clean the outside of the platter." I believe the
principle and the practice of the Gospel in its
spirituality, to be absolutely inseparable whatever may appear.

It is scarcely to be supposed, that a professed
Socinian is present at our communion, offering
divine worship to him whom they believe to be
no more than man, and ascribing to his blood an
atoning power, which they believe not that it
possesses. But many we fear there are, who in
a very similar state of mind, do indeed "eat and
drink their own condemnation, not discerning
the Lord's body," bowing to the outward and
visible sign, of that of which they do not apprehend the inward and spiritual grace. They do,
I believe, as much commit an act of idolatry, as
the Papist who bows before the host; in that
they ascribe to the means the benefits exhibited
in them, and expect from the symbolical ceremony the remission of sins they never con-
siderately and seriously expected from the death
and passion of the Lord Jesus Christ. They

come here once a month, or thrice in the year, to
make up their accounts with the eternal creditor; or rather to wipe out the debts of which
they at least have kept no reckoning, and accre-
dit themselves with him for a score to come; and
this they expect to do, not by application of
the blood of Christ, but by performance of the
ceremony appointed to represent it. They do
exactly what the carnal and corrupted Jew did,
when he induced the Holy One of Israel to say
of his own appointed sacrifices, "Who has required this at your hands? Your new moons
and your appointed feasts my soul hateth." I
believe they do all that the Papist does, when
he receives between his dying lips the consecrated wafer, and believes it a passport to eternal life. They make a Saviour of the means of
grace, and attribute to them that living efficacy
for the remission of sin, and sanctification of
the soul, which resides only in the blood of God,
in the blood of him who was God as well as
man: thus ascribing to the creature the attributes
of Deity;—the essential character of idolatry.
O pause! and before you lay your hand upon
that bread, and wet your lips with that mysterious cup, examine yourselves, what you really
think it is: "Bread and wine, which the Lord
hath commanded to be received." Yes, but do
you believe with equal verity, the thing signified—the blood shed, the body broken, the sole

atonement for a ruined world, the only method of salvation for a sinner—for yourself? That blood, the blood of God, shed by you, shed for you, without which you must have perished, without which, received by faith, you will perish still? That body, the body of your Lord, your risen Lord, seated now on heaven's high throne, there pleading still his sufferings and his merits against your desert of everlasting death? It is not asked if we believe some mysterious property in the bread and wine, imparted to it by God, for the benefit of our souls—if we think that Jesus is really present in them: it is easier to believe a miracle, than to believe the truth; there is scarce a falsehood or absurdity of human invention in religion, that does not find more true believers than the great mystery of godliness, God manifest in the flesh. The question is, do you believe that mystery? Have you examined yourself, whether you do or not? " Jesus knew who they were that believed not," " Not discerning the Lord's body." We must not come here at a venture, and take it for granted that we believe, what no one ever did believe, without a supernatural influence, for "no man can call Jesus Lord, but by the Holy Ghost." This is no thing of course. This is that faith of God's elect, without which we must not presume to eat of this bread, and drink of this cup; pledges of a salvation in which, without such faith, we can have no interest; for "Every spirit that confesseth not that Christ is come in the flesh, is not of God."

But this is not all. There are Pharisees at the Lord's table: these come not from the lanes and hedges; they are the well-dressed guests, who come to buy the Saviour with more worthless coin than Judas sold him for—their own supposed deserving. They do, or rather they did once, require a Saviour, but that was long ago, perhaps before their baptism. Christ has died, and risen, and gone again to heaven, and left the gate open for all that can make their way to its eternal portal. Methinks the Christian Pharisee is worse than they of old: they brought the mint, the anise, and the cummin, the tything of their own: but these have robbed the Lord's garden for their gifts, and bring the benefits of his death as merits of their own, to buy an interest in it. He has given them pardon, grace, and opportunity: they will use these properly, and merit heaven; or—more subtle pride!—will merit him who merited it for them. Such guests as these have taken pains to fit themselves for the communion: they have spent some time, it is likely, in preparation for it, perhaps a week; for I have heard of communicants who put off attending the Sacrament, till they have a leisure week: a temporary abstinence from guilty pleasures and covetous desires, a compulsory sacrifice of prayer, and

reading, and reflection: in short, they have
done what the church commands, examined
themselves; they have confirmed their persuasion of God's undoubted mercy, brought to
remembrance Christ's forgotten death, found
themselves guiltless towards their neighbors,
and having satisfied themselves on all these
points, they bring their persuasion, their good
resolutions, and their harmlessness, to furnish
out the provisions of their master's table, and
while they lay them at his feet, alas, how like
they are to him who came of old, and said,
" What lack I yet?" except, indeed, in his sorrow, for they go away contented, leaving, not
unfrequently their costly dress behind them,
their good resolutions, their remembrance and
contrition, till wanted for the next week's preparation. " Go and sell all that thou hast," for
thou art too rich as yet to follow Christ, or take
this holy Sacrament to your comfort. " We
are not worthy to gather up the crumbs under
thy table." They do not think so. " The remembrance of them is grievous to us, the burden of them is intolerable." They have no
such feeling. " In newness of life;" why new?
they lead very good lives. They were renewed
in baptism. " All these have I kept from my
youth up;" or if not, I have repented, and confessed my sins.—God is merciful, and Christ
has redeemed me and all mankind. Thus con-
fused, in fact, are the minds of many upon the

means of justification before God, and thus uncertain whether they depend for salvation upon
themselves, or God's mercy, or Christ's death,
or any, or all of them together. But such persons are not fit communicants at the Lord's
table; because not having renounced their own
righteousness, they are not prepared to put on
the righteousness of Christ, the wedding garment made for them: and whether their self-
righteousness consists of the graces and virtues
of natural disposition, or assumes the improved
character of Christian obedience, presented as a
title to salvation or depended upon as a means
to it, it is the same ragged and impure garment,
over which the blessed Jesus will not throw the
costly mantle of his own pure merits: most
willing as he is to give it us instead, if these be
first put off.

I have said that in the religion of the Gospel,
principle and practice have no separate reality.
Faith without works is dead—has no real
existence: and works without faith are imprac-
ticable. I do not mean, as assuredly the Apostle never meant, that they co-exist, as mediums
of salvation jointly necessary to the justification
of a sinner. This is denied: because faith only
is the appointed means by which the blood of
Jesus is applied to the justification of the soul,
which becomes eternally complete in Him,
before any good works are or can be done.
But the faith which does nothing towards bring-

12

ing the life into conformity with the Gospel, is
not vital faith—is a creed and not a principle.
Our argument does not go to show that the
believer in Christ may live in ungodliness and
be finally rejected, because he brings forth no
fruit; but that where there is no fruit there is
no principle of faith, and therefore no believer.
The wild grapes do not cause, however they
may prove, the badness of the vine: neither do
the good fruits make good the tree, which had
it not been good before, had never borne them.
I have said, and I think so, that there cannot be
a correct yet unfruitful principle of religion:
but there may be a correct yet barren creed.
For this cause, it is required of them that come
to the Lord's Supper to examine themselves
not only as to their contrition for former sins,
and the reality of their faith in Christ, but as to
their intention to lead a godly and religious life.
" Stedfastly purposing to lead a new life"—no
doubt " the new life"—the life of the renewed,
regenerated soul, created anew in Christ Jesus
unto good works. " If any man be in Christ
he is a new creature." " Grant that we may
hereafter serve and please thee in newness of
life." Here is no boast, no promise; but there
is and must be in every communicant who
approaches this most holy table, the honest
desire, the stedfast purpose, and the believing
prayer, that we may walk hereafter in all God's
holy ways. Have we no unfit communicants

in this particular? Jesus knew who they were
that should betray him; and Satan knew.
And he knows still who they are in every
church communion that say "Lord, Lord; but
do not the things that he says;"—who come to
confess their sins, but not to part with them;
who mean to live hereafter as they have lived
heretofore; and ask the influences of that Spirit,
whose power, if they believe in it, they purpose
to resist. These are that second class whom
we at first defined as they that bring their
unrenounced corruptions into Christ's holy
presence; and do indeed expect and intend, as
far as in them lies, still to retain them when
they go away. Perhaps to the latest hour on
the Saturday night, or trespassing on the opening of the Sabbath, these communicants have
been seen among the assemblies of the wicked,
listening to the profanation of God's sacred
name, conniving at the transgression of his
laws—feeding their vanity or stimulating their
ambition—filling their imagination with unhallowed images, and wilfully bestirring every
ungodly passion. They have been scheming
for their pride, or trafficking for their covetous-
ness; bargaining to sell their gracious Lord for
gold, or something that gold can purchase; and
they intend when the sacrament is over, to
consummate the bargain; they intend for the
world's profits, its pleasures, or its opinions, to
sacrifice his glory and to shame his faith, and

help his enemies to put him out of sight and out
of mind.   Oh! it is an awful moment, when the
sin-loving, earth-devoted communicant, lays
hand upon the sacred emblems; the strengthening of the soul to disobedience—the refreshing
of the spirit to serve another master—the ple-
nary indulgence, not the remedy for sin.   Is it
not the very triumph of the evil one?   " When
he cometh, he findeth it swept and garnished;
then goeth he and taketh to him seven other
spirits more wicked than himself, and they enter
in and dwell there; and the last state of that
man is worse than the first."   " Eat, and drink
their own damnation."   The expression has
been thought too strong; and were it not in the
word of God, charity no doubt, would long
since have expunged it from our ritual.   It has
been certainly misunderstood, so as to beget
much needless and superstitious terror.   We
have before remarked that the reception of the
elements does not beget an obligation which
did not exist before; nor subject the recipient
to a damnation of which he was otherwise in
no danger.   " He that believeth not is condemned already"—not because he eats the
sacramental bread and wine—but " because he
hath not believed in the name of the only-begotten Son of God."

But consider what it is the impenitent and
unbelieving really do on these occasions; and
the words will scarcely seem too strong; that

have not proved strong enough to deter them. They exhibit their full knowledge of God's method of salvation, and give to the terms of it their full consent. They peruse the covenant of grace, and as it were sign it, by which they who are in Christ are saved, they who are not in Christ are lost; and they take into their mouths the appointed signs and pledges, that so it is, and so it shall be; and if the while they have not any consciousness of being lost, or any definite purpose of coming to Christ that they may be saved; any due sense of the guilt of sin, or settled purpose to forsake it; any evidence of a work of grace upon their hearts, or any earnest desire that such a work should appear;—what do they, what can they properly be said to do, but eat and drink their own damnation? put into their mouths the witnesses to God's immutable truth, and their own eternal ruin.

If there is—it is a painful thought—if we must suppose it possible that there should be a believer at the altar, who holds the truth in unrighteousness; who has indulged, and means to indulge, the sins that Jesus died for; who, trusting to be covered with his seamless robe of merit, wears meantime and is content to wear, the garment spotted with the flesh—who loves the freeness of the Gospel, but cannot bear its strictness; would drink the justifying blood, without the purifying water, and feed upon the

12*

flesh, without growing into the likeness of its
purity: if there is a communicant—our terms
will be understood where they apply—who on
some presumptive evidence of sonship, some
by-gone recognitions of a covenant God, and
signs of union and adoption in the Beloved,
does venture with unwashen hands and heart
unsanctified to touch this mysterious food; let
such a one consider what he does. "Can ye
drink the cup of the Lord and the cup of
devils?" We come together to celebrate the
death of Him, in whom, if we died, we died to
sin;—being crucified with Him, that the body
of sin might be destroyed, that henceforth we
might not serve sin. If we be alive in Christ,
it is that our members may be instruments of
righteousness unto God; if we be raised up
with Him from the dead by the glory of the
Father, it is that we may walk in newness of
life.

Reason there is for all to hear the church's
warning—lest we eat and drink our own condemnation; provoking Him to plague us with
divers diseases and sundry kinds of death; to
heat the furnace of affliction seven times hotter;
and lay the hand of judgment seven-fold hea-
vier; and swell to a frightful torrent this gentle
stream of love, in which we affect to drink
while we refuse to wash. Most tender and indulgent Father! thy children will know in heaven, perhaps, how often they have done this—

how often met·thee here, thy right hand full of blessings, but by reason of some cherished sin that they have brought with them, forced thee to exchange it for a rod; to throw some bitter medicament into the cup of life, or hide thy face from the polluting imagery of last night's revelry, or to-morrow's strife, pursuing them to the very footstool of thy throne.

CHAPTER VIII.

W<small>HY</small> are ye so fearful?—how is it that ye have no faith? When Jesus beholds the trembling step and sinking heart, the smouldering hope and scarcely smouldering expectation, with which his people come to take his blessings, and sees also how little blest they seem to go away—surely if he did not remember whereof we are made—if he were not " touched with a feeling of our infirmities "—surely He would not spread his table any more, for guests so little hungry when they come—so little satisfied when they depart! It is no fault of his, " For what could he have done more for his vineyard than he has not done." He bought it at no ordinary price even no less than his own precious blood. With all the glory he had before the world began, with all the riches of his Father's throne, with all the fulness of his own eternal Godhead, relinquished, put aside:—with poverty and shame, and mortal anguish, a broken body and a broken heart, He bought this little vineyard. Oh how he must have loved it! And when He had bought it, he had it not—he paid the price, but another was in possession, and

Jesus had to conquer what he had bought so
dear. There was not an entrance but was
barred against him, and sin, and death and hell
were at the gates! Do we say *were* there?
They are there still! Step by step, one by
one, the blessed Lord has had to win his own;
his own unwilling, resisting, refusing:—" Behold, I stand at the door and knock." By patient and long-suffering p'ty; by warnings forgotten and promises disbelieved; by his disputed
word, by his resisted Spirit, by his despised and
persecuted servants; by patient pleadings of un-
requited love, and ceaseless prayers before the
Father's throne, the Saviour conquers out his
scant inheritance, and brings to submission a re-
luctant people. Oh! think if he does not love
them! And does his work end here? When
he has bought, and conquered, and entered into
possession—when he has fenced it and planted
it, and hedged it round, and built a tower in the
midst—in the communion of his separated
church, in the little company of his regenerate
people, does the blessed Redeemer come into his
fair garden to see the grapes cluster and the
wine-press flowing, and find all fruitfulness and
beauty round him?

No. His purchase is a spot of sterile earth;
his conquest is an untamed wilderness. It is
like those fastnesses of unknown lands which
earthly princes sell or give away to whoever
can find or conquer them: they must fell the

forest before they can have a dwelling-place, or
gather any harvest of their fields. More easy
task! for these at least find materials for their
work. But Jesus, when he comes into the
heart, finds nothing—nothing but what is against
him; perverted intellect, and adverse habits, and
preoccupied affections: full, full to the very extremity of things inimical. In a pestilent air
and an ungracious soil, the Saviour cultivates
his precious garden; precious indeed, if valued
by its cost; most precious, if by the love he has
manifested for it. By his word, too slowly
learned; by his Spirit, too often grieved; by
judgments provoked and blessings undervalued,
and opportunities and ordinances neglected, this
never-wearied husbandman plies his loving toil.
For a confiding, trusting, and rejoicing people?
No! Let the heart of every believer answer for
itself, what sort of love does love like this
beget? Suspicious, anxious, apprehensive;
wanting fresh proofs of love so dearly proved;
and when he grants them, doubting, doubting
still: doubting, lest he who loved should change
his mind, and rid himself of his too costly purchase. Oh, if its worthlessness could do it;—if
ill-requiting could have changed it—if he had
not from all eternity foreseen that those he died
for, would be afraid to trust him, and borne
upon his cross this deadliest sin of all; he never
need have left his Father's throne, for not a
sinner had been saved! We do not know—

but I could think, for Jesus was a man—
that on that night in which he was betrayed,
at that funereal supper—so sad, so sorrowful;
I could think it was not the treachery of Judas
that was heaviest on him; for Judas was none
of his, he was not about to expiate Judas' sin:
Peter's denial, and Thomas's unbelief, and the
strife, and cowardice, and abandonment of all,
were in the Saviour's thoughts, when he took
bread, and brake it, and gave it to his disciples. And if the eye of his omniscient Godhead looked at that moment through the extent
of time, and saw in every future communion of
his saints, how few would justly estimate his
love, or come in full assurance of his truth;
what fearful, unwilling, unconfiding communicants would come, what unblest, uncomforted,
unthankful ones would go away; surely had his
love been any thing less than infinite, it would
have died before it cost him life! Our subject
overbears us; I wished to take some measure
of the Saviour's love, I wished to express the
little I can think of its immeasurable greatness.
But I have failed, I have said less than I know,
which yet is all but as a drop to the unbounded
ocean. Perhaps it is like the traveller's first
vision of the distant Alps, he is only sure he
sees them, and that they as much exceed his
expectations, as they exceed all other things he
sees.

Such a one is He who has made a supper, and

bade many—bade all; for as there is but one
name under which salvation is offered to mankind—the name of sinner—he amongst us who
cannot claim that title, alone can say he has received no invitation. But because Jesus knows
whereof we are made; the mortal darkness of
our spiritual sense, our inaptness to perceive the
things unseen, and keep in mind what only faith
lays hold of, he has clothed in sensible images
eternal things, making outward and visible signs
a means of intercourse between Himself who is
a spirit, and man who is but dust. "To the end
that we should always remember the exceeding
great love of our Master and only Saviour Jesus
Christ, thus dying for us, and the innumerable
benefits which by his precious blood-shedding
he hath obtained to us; he hath instituted and
ordained holy mysteries, as pledges of his love,
and for a continual remembrance of his death,
to our great and endless comfort." The terms
in which we are bidden to the sacramental ceremony, are the same in which we are invited to
the cross of Christ; our title to partake of it is
the same as our title to the benefits of his death.
The preparation on our part is the same, the fitness the same, the state of mind the same, and
the perceptible effects the same, as required of
them who come to Christ: and the exclusion, if
either we come not, or coming not aright, be
finally cast out, will be in either case the same.
"Ye will not come unto me that ye might have

life;"—" not discerning the Lord's body;"—
" not having on a wedding garment."

Viewing the Sacrament thus, I cannot contemplate the necessity of a ceremonial preparation for it. The state in which a believer habitually lives is the state in which he is required to appear at the table; and there is no moment of our spiritual course in which we can safely be unfit for the worthy receiving of the bread and wine. I mean safely as to our own perception of our condition in Jesus Christ. *Who* is safe in the eternal purpose of the Most High, *whose* name is written where there never shall be found a blot, is God's own secret; the believer reads his name, his new name, written on the fleshly tablets of a regenerated heart; he sees it, as we see the star of night upon the clear smooth waters; no vague uncertain indication of what is reflected from above, though liable to be darkened by intervening clouds, or broken by the perturbation of the waters. We know it will be answered in favor of a preparation, that the state of a Christian is no such definite thing; the greater number of those who come and ought to come to the Lord's table, are of doubtful minds whether they be in Christ or not—whether or not they are living a life of faith, and walking not after the flesh but after the Spirit. This indeed is more true than it ought to be; and it is far from my desire to discountenance self-examination. " Examine yourselves whether ye be

13

in the faith:" " Give diligence to make your
calling and election sure." Indeed, however
sure it is, however firm the believer stands upon
the rock of ages, Christian assurance is not of
that kind, that needs no renewed examination.
It is not a bold and fearless confidence, that
having once upon sufficient evidence realised
our interest in the death of Christ, and our union
with him, has no further occasion to look into
our security. There is too much within, and
too much without, to shake the believer's faith
and cloud his confidence, to admit of such a state.
Safe he is, and safe he knows himself to be, for
he has built his house upon a rock: but when
the waters break beneath, and the tempest black-
ens above, he casts many an inquiring look upon
the firm foundation on which his hopes are
stayed. The most assured believer is only sure,
because every inquiry brings the same gracious
promise back; every fresh examination unfolds
new proofs of Jesus' faithfulness and love, every
fear that sin awakens, or Satan whispers, is allayed by the renewed witness of the indwelling
Spirit. The church as well as the Scriptures
requires all who " do mind to come to the
Lord's table to *examine* themselves," but in
neither is it said to *prepare* themselves. And I
know that those persons whose indeterminate
character, or unstable faith, or habitual infirmities
of the flesh, keep them in uncertainty as to their
acceptance with the Father, and union with the

Son, and vitality in the Spirit, are exactly the persons most likely to delude or to enslave themselves by what is called a preparation;—to mistake for principle a superindnced emotion, and trust their faith to periodical revivals.

Few things can be more adverse to a genuine growth in grace, than such a fitful culture, leaving to prolonged sterility the exhausted soil, and to speedy distaste the questionable fruits. We will even suppose a case, in which a season of preparation might seem the most necessary for the recovery of a right state of mind preparatory to the feast. Let it be, for example, the case of a Christian, whose mind has been so much occupied during the past weeks, that he has not had time to think about the condition of his soul, to realise his faith and penitence, or examine the state of his spiritual affections: and he hesitates in this condition to approach the Lord's table. Now this absorption of feeling in the things of time, has been wilful, or it has been providential. If wilful, nothing can be more injurious, than to suppose it may go on with certain or uncertain intervals of devotional leisure preparatory to the Sacrament. When it has unhappily occurred, it is to be deeply repented and deprecated for all time to come; not compensated by a week of preparation: this were indeed to live without God in the world, three weeks out of four. If on the contrary, the pressure of occupation has been unusual and providential, I know no kinder

interposition of divine love for the healing and
refreshing of the soul, than this Sacrament itself,
no sweeter rest from the enforced labor, no holier, fitter opportunity to retrieve the unwilling
declension of spiritual life. When can the hungry soul be so well prepared to feed, as when it
has been long obliged to fast? When hasten to
the fount with so much zest, as when the scorch-
ing sun and thirsty soil have drunk up all the
streams? "Come unto me all ye that are weary
and heavy-laden"—weary of earth's toils, and
laden with its unwilling cares. Do not wait to
appease your hunger, and sate your thirst before
you come—the table is spread and the provision
free; "Take, eat," to the strengthening and refreshing of your souls.

If it be necessary to consider another case, a
still more painful case, to contemplate a period
in the Christian's life, in which he who has been
used to take these elements to his great and endless comfort, has lost the witness of the Spirit
within him—lost the evidences of his title to
partake of them; a period when he does *not*
repent him of his former sins, believe the promises of God in Jesus Christ, or purpose to walk
henceforth in the way of his commandments—
that soul is in a position of misery and danger
in which it cannot pause: there is more to do
than to prepare for the Sacrament. The backslider has to make again his calling and election
sure; to go again, as at the first, a contrite pro-

digal to his father's house. For whatever he
may have heretofore enjoyed, however sure he
may heretofore have been of his acceptance, he
can keep neither the joy nor the assurance, while
he lives apart and defiles the temple of the Holy
Ghost. "I am no more worthy to be called thy
son." Again he must assume the publican's
part, for the seal of adoption is hidden on his
brow. Happy if there be enough of memory
left, to stimulate and encourage him to return.
If this be the mind of such an one, under a full
sense of his defection, self-known, and self-con-
demned. I do not know why the altar where
the pledges of pardon and reconciliation are exhibited, should be an unfit place to throw himself
again upon his Father's mercy, and receive again
the tokens of forgiveness. But if the backslider
be of another mind; if he feel no anguish, no
compunction, no determination to leave his wan-
derings and return to God—we have spoken to
this case before—he must not come at all—no
preparation can make him fit to come, till grace
has broken his heart.

I cannot but think, and it is the bearing of
much that I have said, that there is a misappre-
hension in the minds of many Christians respecting the nature of this rite, injuriously affecting
those who come, only less than those whom it
unreasonably keeps away. It is not contem-
plated as a feast of love, a memorial exclusively
of mercy. "Ye are not come unto the mount
13*

that might be touched, and that burned with fire, nor unto blackness, and darkness, and tempest."

Our Christian communion is not one of those bloody sacrifices of the law, whereby was "remembrance again made of sins every year," neither an offering "of those gifts and sacrifices that could not make him that did the service perfect, as pertaining to the conscience." It is not even an exhibition of the wrath of God in the death of the only-begotten Son, to alarm the sinner, and impress upon the conscience the inevitable consequences of unforgiven sin. For if it were, a quite different company should be called together: the careless, the impenitent, the unbelieving, would be the fittest communicants, whose presence is now forbidden. No, if we are called at this gracious time to the remembrance of our sins, it is only to enhance the love that, far as the east is from the west, has put our iniquities from us. If we are made to confess them, it is only as 'a reckoning kept of debts that another pays, to estimate the sum we owe —of gratitude to the forgiver, not of penalty to the exacter of his dues. Unexpiated and unforgiven sin, justice and judgment and everlasting death, are not brought into sight at all by this exhibition of the death of Christ—else why are none bidden, but they who are pardoned, reconciled, and born anew; of whom the word says, "that they shall not come into judgment;"—of whom Christ has said, "that they shall never die!" This is no outer-court, where strangers stand, and servants wait, and criminals expect their arraignment, and petitioners the rejection of their suit. It is not for me to say what company the King of Kings, and Lord of Lords beholds, when he comes at these set times, to sit between the cherubim on the mercy seat: the veil of the sanctuary undrawn; neither what he foresaw when he said at the first communion, " There are some among you that believe not:" —" Ye are not all clean." But by all the conversation that He held at that first supper, by all his loving words, and provident cares, and strong assurances, I judge it is no such assembly he addresses or has provided for in the richness of the blessings he bestows. "Henceforth I call ye not servants"—"but I have called you friends." " If ye abide in me, and my words abide in you, ye shall ask what ye will, and it shall be done unto you." " As the Father hath loved me, so have I loved you." " These things have I spoken to you that my joy might remain in you, and that your joy might be full." " Greater love hath no man than this, that a man lay down his life for his friends." " If a man love me, he will keep my words; and my Father will love him; and we will come unto him and make our abode with him. Ye have not chosen me, but I have chosen you, that ye should bring forth much fruit, and that

your fruit should remain." "Peace I leave
with you, my peace I give unto you. Let not
your heart be troubled, neither let it be afraid."
"These things have I spoken to you, that ye
might have peace; in the world ye shall have
tribulation; but be of good cheer, I have overcome the world." This, and such as this is the
language of the blessed Jesus to his first communicants; and through them to all who should
thereafter eat of his flesh and drink his blood, in
faithful repetition of the ceremony. Here is no
mention of death, and judgment, and the wrath
to come; even the wrath and condemnation past
are out of sight, buried in promises of peace
and love. In similar language would he now
address us; in similar language does he now address us through the administration of his feast.
"Hear what comfortable words our Saviour
Christ said to all that truly turn unto him,
'Come unto me, all that travail and are heavy
laden, and I will refresh you.'" "So God loved
the world that he gave his only-begotten Son, to
the end that all that believe in him should not
perish, but have everlasting life." "Take, eat,
this is my body which was broken for you—
this is my blood which was shed for you."
Can this be the mysterious imagery that scares
the trembling sinner from the table, and sinks
the heart of the penitent as he approaches?
"Lift up the hands that hang down, and
strengthen the feeble knees." A mystery it is—

worthy, by its impassable distance from all
finite comprehension, to be the plan and purpose of the Infinite; but in the palpable exhibition and design, and adaptation of it, as ob-
vious, as apprehensible, as food is to the appetite, as rest is to the weary, as peace is to the
troubled, as love is to the longings and achings
of the soul.

Gracious King! Princes of this world when
they make a feast for their brethren and friends,
and such as have the privilege of their chamber,
do never meet so sad a company as thine. They
too may find an enemy disguised, a traitor con-
cealed among the visitors; but they will not
meet with such strange friends as thou dost!
so loath to show themselves, so doubtful of
their welcome, so suspicious and mistrustful of
thy favor; uncertain between a blessing and a
curse. The favored subject knows his opportunity, the adopted brother expects a brother's
welcome, the children of the household look for
royal gifts. Nay, we may go lower than this
to shame our cold expectancy. " The ox know-
eth his owner, and the ass his master's crib, but
my people do not know,"—they hesitate, they
doubt, they turn away disconsolate from my
tokens of affection. " Reach hither thy finger,
and behold my hands, and reach hither thy
hand, and thrust it into my side: and be not
faithless, but believing."

Never, I think, may we so fully realise the

actual presence of the Redeemer, in all the sym-
pathising attributes of his manhood, as in this
little communion of his saints, when the doors
are closed upon the unbelieving world, and all
but himself and his are supposed to be shut out.
As in his risen body upon earth, he was invisible to all but those who had loved him, and
accepted him in the flesh, so here when the
door is shut, and only the disciples pray within,
we may behold Jesus standing in the midst,
manifesting himself to us as he does not to the
world. The world may contemplate a distant
God, a first Creator, an unseen Ruler, and a
future Judge. The disciples of Jesus only can
behold in Deity the Son of Man; hold converse
with Deity in a nature like their own, and
recieve the gifts of Deity from a brother's hand.

I have said something in discouragement of a
ceremonial preparation of the Lord's Supper;
but there is a preparation more suitable. " He
that descended is the same also that ascended
up far above all heavens, that he might fill all
things." The same Jesus whose death and
passion we commemorate, sits now on heaven's
throne, the sole distributor of heaven's gifts.
" Wherefore he saith, when he ascended up on
high, he led captivity captive, and gave gifts to
men." Surely if there be a time above every
other time in which this enthroned Giver's
hand is full of the costly purchases of his suffering, it must be when he comes to commemorate

the price at which he bought them; comes in to
sup—it is his own familiar word—with the elect
members of his body upon earth. The most
suitable preparation for such a time of largess,
I think is to be ready with our wants; to prepare our requests, to determine what we will
have of all that he comes laden with to distribute. I think that we should be prepared, at
each returning season of administration, with
the immediate and individual wants that are
most pressing on us at the time. If there is
some sin that we have struggled hard against,
and have not conquered, some duty we have
not found strength or spirit to perform; if there
is some fear upon our souls, or apprehensive
dread of things to come; if any sorrow, deeper
than mortal ken, unreached by mortal sympathy—any difficulty, any impossibility—nay, for
I must not stop short—if there be a shame that
dares not show itself to earthly eyes, a remorse
that earthly judgment would not pity—if
Uriah's image be graven upon David's heart,
or the false oath still sound on Peter's lips—
with these, even all of these let the penitent
believer make himself ready, furnish himself
out, take them in his hand, against the moment
when in the midst of the banquet the king shall
hold out the golden sceptre and say, " What is
thy petition and it shall be granted thee? What
is thy request and it shall be performed?"
Here let the father bring his profligate child,

and here the wife her unbelieving husband, and here the persecuted saint his enemies; and say again the long-repeated prayer, and ask again the still-ungranted boon. It has been done—has it been ever done in vain? Month after month the communicant of a sorrowful spirit has been seen—seen of the Lord, mistaken of all beside, wondered at, perhaps rebuked—"Why weepest thou, why eatest thou not, why is thy soul grieved?" "She spake in her heart, only her lips moved, but her voice was not heard." The same besetting sin, the same abiding sorrow, the same overwhelming want still holden forward in the suppliant hand. "Out of the abundance of my complaint and grief have I spoken hitherto." There has seemed no acceptance, but never a repulse—no answer, perhaps, but an encouraging smile, that seemed to say, Come again; until she that came long in bitterness of soul, has come at last in joy, and gone her way, her countenance no more sad. 1 Sam. i, 1.

CHAPTER IX.

"Whatsoever things ye desire when ye pray, believe that ye receive them, and ye shall have them." It is a strong expression, but it is the word of him who knew what he required, and for what he undertook. The promise is without limitation, but the required faith is of no common kind. It is not the belief that God *can* do for us whatsoever we ask; it is not the common persuasion that God heareth prayer, and may be intreated by us. There is a reach of faith, not only far beyond this, but beyond even the more definite belief, or rather hope, that it may please God at any special time to grant us our request, which supports the believer in his time of need, and is usually sufficient to that end: for it seems to be the merciful provision of God for our weak estate, that the soul can feed on hope, when faith is not strong enough to taste assurance. But our Lord proposes more. St. John carries this out when he says, " This is the confidence we have in him, that if we ask anything according to his will, he heareth us: and if we know that he hear us, whatsoever we ask

14

we know that we have the petitions that we desired of him." Such was the confidence of Elias, when " He prayed fervently that it might not rain, and it rained not on the earth by the space of three years and six months." It was the confidence of Hannah, when, before she saw the accomplishment of her wishes, otherwise than by the eye of faith, she went away and did eat. It was the faith of the centurion, when it was said to him, " As thou believest, so be it done unto thee," and he went away satisfied with the reply. How often, or must I say how seldom such a faith is in exercise when we pray, we must answer to ourselves; but we shall never find that where the condition has been fulfilled, the undertaking of our Lord has fallen short. It is no discouragement that there is a reservation of God's will, and the suppliant cannot certainly know if the petition be according to his will or not. In especial cases, such as those of Elijah and Hannah, there was no doubt a divine intimation to the soul, that such was the will of God, as I suppose there always is, when such a faith is exercised in prayer for any temporal object, not comprehended in the general promises: the prayer and the belief are both of God, a prelude and indication of his acceptance of them.— But the greater, and by far the most important part of the things we seek of God in prayer, are those in which there is no doubt about his will. " He willeth not that any should perish, but that

all should come to the knowledge of the truth."
" This is the will of God, even your sanctification." " This is the will of him that sent me,
that every one which seeth the Son, and believeth
on him, may have everlasting life." In all that
affects the welfare of the soul, in all our spiritual
petitions, the will of God is certainly known.—
For pardon, holiness, and peace; for faith, and
hope, and charity; for application of the blood
of Christ, the outpouring of the Holy Spirit, the
glory of the Father in us, and by our means,
against temptation, and all manner of sin, against
the world, the flesh, and the Devil, we pray with
no uncertainty of the will of God; though even
for these things he will be inquired of, not to induce his willingness, but to manifest our own.
With reference to things merely temporal, there
are general promises and declarations of God's
will, quite as unlimited as the eternal promises,
such as the " all things needful—no good thing
withheld—no want of any manner of thing that
is good; no sparrow falling to the ground uncared
for—no hair of the head unnumbered." To
this extent, even in earthly good, the reservation
of God's will is no impediment to believing
prayer, for wherever there is promise, there may
be the full exercise of faith upon it. In more
definite desires, for which there is no special promise, and man in his ignorance cannot know
whether or not they be included in these general
ones, because he does not know if they be good;

there is still no more reservation in the promise
than will be always in the wise man's prayer,
and in the desire of the believing heart. We do
not wish them, we would in no wise have them
in opposition to our Maker's will. If, when we
ask an egg, our heavenly Father knows it would
prove a scorpion to us, we do not mean to urge
the unconditional suit, and have it granted at all
ventures. "Whatsoever" then—let us repeat the
gracious words, "whatsoever things ye desire
when ye pray, believe that ye receive them, and
ye shall have them."

If this were realised, what treasure-laden
guests would leave the Saviour's table—what
gladdened eyes and throbbing hearts. Let us
look over the petitions we have offered, and
suppose for a moment they have all been granted. "For thy Son our Lord Jesus Christ's sake,
forgive us all that is past:"—"Pardon and deliver you from all your sins:"—"Not weighing
our merits but pardoning our offences." Those
offences so grievous to remember, those sins so
intolerable to us to bear, all pardoned, all removed, and all in immutable promise overcome;
our sinful bodies made clean by his body, our
souls washed in his most precious blood. "Grant
that we may ever hereafter serve and please
thee in newness of life." "Confirm and strength-
en you in all goodness." "That all we who are
partakers of this holy communion, may be fulfilled with thy heavenly benediction." "So to

assist us with thy grace, that we may continue in that holy fellowship, and do all such good works as thou hast prepared for us to walk in."
Holiness, devotedness, conformity to the mind and will of God, for which our hearts have failed with longing, and our strength is gone with struggling, are here all pledged, and granted to our prayers; the good works prepared for us to do—the grace bestowed sufficient to the doing of them, not by our poor measurement of what we require, or God requires of us; but by his own eternal provision for our happiness and his glory, in the way of his commandments. "And bring you to everlasting life." " That we may evermore dwell in him and he in us." The end secured as well as the means provided, God's glory and honor pledged for our everlasting life; our fears and doubts about the issue all allayed; and every insufficiency or mutability of ours, provided against by immediate and eternal union with the all-sufficient, immutable Son of God. "He in me, and I in you; the things that I do, ye shall do also."

We have recalled these few of our public and general petitions, made special as they should have been by every communicant for himself, and applied to the immediate pressure of his wants; and we say, that to believing prayer every one of these petitions has been granted, and is to be realised according to the specific bearing of our prayers. For as different images

14*

are made use of to designate different wants—
hunger and thirst and sickness and weariness,
with each its own provision: so at the spiritual
banquet there is a distribution suited to the appetite of every separate guest. We need only
to know our wants, and take our own prepared
portion. For example, there are times when
the desire for pardon so overbears every other
wish, nothing else can be relished, and the cry
for mercy can alone be raised. There are other
times when pardon is so assured as to be lost
sight of in yearnings after the sanctification of
the Spirit. Sometimes it is the past, and sometimes the present, and sometimes the future that
weighs most upon us; sometimes our own cares,
and sometimes our care for others. The provident master has foreseen all this, and spreads his
multiplied provisions out, and bids us take our
choice. The grateful, and satisfied, and rejoicing
guest should go away feeling that he receives
the especial object of his prayers. I say especial, because I think we lose by sinking in general petitions for what is always needful, the
recollection and solicitation of our immediate
and more sensible desires. Prepared with these
desires, furnished with our wants, our miseries,
and our sins, if we go in holy confidence to the
table, expecting to receive our portion at the
Saviour's hand; it is due to his love, his honor,
and his truth, that we come not away disconsolate, dissatisfied, desponding. The faith that

suffices to take us to our knees, proves sometimes insufficient to outlast the prayer: and they
who come in faith to seek a boon, go away
without any persuasion of having obtained it.
Yet this is not the divine injunction. "Believe
that ye receive them," and it is not the Apostle's
experience only, "We know that we have the
petitions that we desired of him." Believe then,
when you leave the sacramental feast, that you
have verily and indeed eaten of the life-giving
flesh, and drunk of the atoning, purifying blood;
and as he that has eaten feels his strength renewed, and he that has drunk feels refreshed, so
perceptible and so assured will be the replenish-
ment of the spiritual life. We have met our
Lord in the place of his appointment. We have
been admitted to the chosen company of his
friends—been welcomed as his brethren, even
as the elect members of his own body. We
have asked of him, at this season of near communion and preferential love, whatsoever we
desired in our hearts; and we have not been, if
we have asked believing, we cannot have been,
refused. Are we startled by this proposition?
Do our thoughts revert to times when we have
asked and had not; have repeated day by day,
it may be, year by year, the unaccepted prayer,
till Satan has seemed to mock our pertinacity,
and moved our hearts to say that God has failed.
Oh! we can all recal such times, with their soul-
sinking bitterness, the malignant triumph of the

powers of darkness, and the relaxing hold of an almost expiring faith.

Perhaps we all know how such a memory comes like a black spirit athwart our prayers, at the very moment when faith is about to realise the promise, and take the blessing home. For surely the great enemy knows—however we may doubt it, and no mortal ear may hear it— he knows that at the moment believing prayer goes up, the grant from heaven is sure, and he puts forth his utmost power to mar such prayers, by injecting sudden doubts and painful recollections. Presumption!—delusion!—the thought darts like a flash of lightning across our minds, and the vision is obscured, and the petition halts, and faith draws back, and doubt takes the place of confidence. Happy, if the suppliant at such a time can say, " An enemy hath done this." An enemy has done it, for such a prayer, if he should let it pass, would shake his throne beneath him. " Get thee behind me, Satan!" is the reply of one who understands the artifice.

But the inexperienced believer, perhaps, will say, " This is no exercise of the imagination. If it be said to us at the altar, " Go in peace, be ye warmed, and be ye filled," and we find ourselves famished and naked as we came, how can we exercise faith upon imaginary gifts, and believe we have what we have not? And is it not, after all, a fact, that we have frequently sought God in vain?" We say it is not a fact, because we know it cannot be. It is in reason, in revelation, and in experience impossible, that God should refuse any thing good to them that are in Jesus Christ. Is it reasonable—is it in common sense supposable—does not God himself condescend to use this most definitive argument, "He that spared not his own son, but delivered him up for us all, how shall he not with him also freely give us all things?" "If when we were enemies, we were reconciled to God by his death, much more, being reconciled, shall we be saved by his life." When Christ has so loved us, and so bought us, and by so much labor made us willing, is it possible that there should be found at last unwillingness in him, or indifference that we perish in his hands. If I should say of things in earth or heaven, what seems to me the most inconceivable impossibility, it is that any sinner should perish who trusts to be saved by Christ in the way appointed for salvation. But lest it should be—as he well knew it would be—that his people manifest towards him an unreasonableness of mistrust we should scarcely exercise toward a fellow man who loved us; approaching him as one so unwilling to do what he has died for, that we must win him, or persuade him, or by extraordinary means induce him to be gracious, and never to the last, be confident of success—in order that we might have strong consolation, who have fled to Christ for refuge—the revealed word, in which it is impossible for God to lie, has been made to say the utmost that can be said, to secure our confidence, and remove our fears. We need not here appeal to it, for every reader of the Scripture knows how ample, how direct, how unconditional are the promises it contains. I repeat it unconditional, for there is not a condition appended to the gift of salvation that is not comprehended in it, that is not a part of it; whether it be repentance, or faith, or prayer, or perseverance, or obedience unto holiness, all are the free gift of God, and the purchase of Jesus' blood; all constitute one whole salvation, provided, not demanded; bestowed, and not exacted: the wedding garment made ready at the feast, with which we have nothing to do, except to put it on. " Put ye on the Lord Jesus Christ," a garment like his own mysterious vesture, in which there is no seam, and shall never be a rent; nothing that has been added, and nothing that can be separated.

If the doubting communicant reverts from reason and revelation to dwell again upon experience; if he says again, " but I have eaten this bread and drunk this wine, and heard the precious promises, and seen these gracious pledges, and I am only where I was; my faith is no stronger, my hopes are no brighter, my sins have still the same dominion over me, my sorrow still lies heavy at my heart; my con-

science is as uneasy, and my soul as unsanctified as ever. I have been to the Sacrament,
and taken it faithfully, but I feel none of the
benefits to be received thereby." I think, then,
that self-examination is as necessary after the
Sacrament, as it is before, lest we charge God
foolishly with unkept promises, and pledges un-
redeemed.

When we go to a physician for our bodies'
health, and receive from him an assurance of
recovery, there are certain things expected of
us to that issue. He requires that we give him
time—that we come as often as he thinks
proper—that we confide in him to choose his
remedies, and to choose the order and method
of applying them; and above all that we follow
his directions: these are indispensable conditions
—not by which we may go and cure ourselves,
but by which we consent to let him cure us.
Similar are the conditions of the sacramental
benefits. We examined ourselves before we
came upon some part of them, whether we
really knew that we were sick and really desired
to be made whole, and truly believed that Christ
could do it for us; we sought out as far as we
could discern the symptoms and pains of our
disorder, that we might lay all before him; and
we determined to commit ourselves to his care.
These were the conditions, the only preparation
required of them who minded to come to the
Lord's table; and these have been complied

with. But what have we done since? Have
we consented that the Lord should take his
time; or because we were not instantly relieved,
begun to doubt his willingness and power?
Have we returned as often as he requires; or
has every little matter of convenience or incon-
venience deferred our visits, and made us fail
of our appointments? if indeed we have not
deliberately and systematically determined that
four times a year is quite enough for all the
benefits we expect to receive from this holy
communion of the body and blood of our
Saviour Christ. Perhaps we have quarrelled
with his remedies, and disputed about the means
wherewith he has proposed to work the cure;
have thought salvation by faith alone a dangerous experiment, better not exhibited unmixed with the sanctions of the law: and when
it is unfolded to us that all shall be of grace,
have even doubted the justice and wisdom of
the scheme: or proposed at least some caution
in the administration of such venturous truths;
some modifications and reserves in our acceptance of them. In short, have we not minded
us of some better way to conquer our sins and
cultivate our graces, and bring to salvation the
objects of our solicitude, than that which the
Gospel scheme proposes and the Word reveals?
Few of us know perhaps to the full extent,
how difficult it is to be honest in our prayers;
and to desire at all cost the thing that we intreat

for; and to consent on our own behalf or that
of those we pray for, to the cutting off the right-
hand or the casting away of the right-eye, by
which alone the skilful chirurgeon can preserve
the life, and bring us to health and peace. Sure
I am that many an ardent prayer has been
given to the winds, because we would have the
grant in some way of our own devising; and
many a longed for blessing been delayed, waiting our consent to the conditions of it. Most
eminently is this the case in respect of spiritual
blessings, seldom conferred in any eminent
degree without a proportionate sacrifice of things
that nature clings to of this world's treasures,
its pomp, its pride, and its opinions—or dearer
still, some treasure of our own, our wisdom or
knowledge or mental independence. Let us
examine ourselves. When we ate that bread
and drank that cup in earnest hope that
Christ should dwell in us, and we in him, were
we agreed that he should cast out of our hearts
all company unsuited to his presence, all that
we could not take with us into union with
himself?

Above all, let the communicant examine
himself whether he leaves his Saviour's presence intending, as far as in him lies, to follow
the directions given him for the attainment of
the blessings he has desired honestly and asked
in faith. Of course—nay, not so much of course
—for if man is such a stultified bewildered crea-

15

ture that he does not always want the thing he asks, nor consent to the thing he prays for, how likely that he will not pursue the very thing he .wants. Let the disappointed communicant who has asked and not received, has eaten and not been strengthened, has drunk, and not felt himself refreshed—who returns month by month, or week by week, to the ceremony, and finds that he becomes no happier, no holier, no more at peace with God and detached from this world's cares, let him follow out this examination of himself; what he does, what he means to do, when he leaves the holy feast. It is a wide inquiry; for while there was but one way in which the good seed fell aright and brought forth its hundred fold, there were three ways in which it became abortive and brought no fruit to perfection: and the ways are so many in which the work of salvation may be hindered and the Holy Spirit grieved, that we can suggest but a few in which we consider the benefits of the Sacrament may be lost by those who have worthily received it: not under extraordinary temptations and assaults of the adversary, by which we may be surprised and forcibly robbed of our treasures, but under circumstances, voluntary and habitual, and apparently consented to on our part. First consider how you intend to pass the remainder of the day, after thus feeding in faith upon the body and blood of Christ: not, of course, for we speak of those who profess the name of Christ—not, I must suppose, to profane the Sabbath by open violation of its sanctity—by taking drives, or paying visits, or receiving company, or reading newspapers, or making preparations for to-morrow's business, or recurring to the work of yesterday. There is a class of communicants who do even this: but we do not suppose them comprehended in the number who have received the same *worthily*—since they have not so much as intended to follow the commandments of God, walking from henceforth in his holy ways.

But even Christians do sometimes at the very door of the sanctuary renew their worldly conversation, or their worldly thoughts; and before the impression of what they have felt has been deepened into permanence—before, if we may so speak, the ink is dry with which their grant of blessings has been signed—wipe off every trace of it from their minds; how hardly afterwards to renew it, and call back the impermanent form of heavenly blessedness they just remember to have seen: while faith and hope and joy go vainly searching for the manna which the sun has melted before they gathered it up, and wait famishing the next day's shower. Are there not Christians also, who, having brought the burthen of their earthly cares to cast it on the Lord, do forget or refuse to leave it there; and resuming the burden as if it were still their

own, before the doors of the sanctuary are well
closed behind them, begin to groan afresh under
the weight, and calculate again the difficulties,
and sinking under this new trial of their strength,
are tempted to question the Almighty, why he
has failed to lighten it? He never proposed to
lighten it—he offered to take it from you, and
carry it himself, but you refused to leave it; and
you mean to resume to-morrow your week-day
cares, What shall I eat, and what shall I drink,
and wherewithal shall I be clothed; pull down
the barns and build greater; bring in provisions
for the days to come; look to the door, for the
thief is coming; look to the moth, for the garment waxeth old; between the hope of getting,
and the fear of losing, not a moment of time is
there to recollect that you made these cares over
to your heavenly Father, and received a promise
in return of all things needful for you. We remember!—But did he exactly mean, we were
to take no thought, to be careful for nothing?—
Yes, he meant it, but you did not; you never
meant to try if he would keep his word. If it
be answered that this earthliness and carefulness
ness of spirit was the very sickness of which we
desire to be healed, the symptoms of our disease
cannot be urged against us, as a reason why we
do not recover, although they be mournful evidences of the fact. This may be true, and often
is true, when, wearied and ashamed of its anx-
ieties, the soul commits itself to God for strength

against such infirmities. But then, has our acting, after the Sacrament, been as honest as our desire before it, and our petitions in it? Have we followed, or even honestly and truly meant to follow the direction of the physician for the subduing of this soul-consuming sickness? Some of his precepts will readily occur. " Be content with such things as ye have—covet not uncertain riches—study to be quiet and do your own business—the servant of the Lord must not strive—seekest thou high things for thyself, seek them not—make not provision for the flesh to fulfil the lusts thereof—ye ask and receive not, because ye ask amiss, that ye may consume it on your lusts." Are those whose spiritual growth is stayed by earthly care and their prayers for peace unanswered, not seeking more of earth than God has promised, more than is needful—not meddling more with earth than their lawful business requires, more than is wholesome—not mingling, more than duty and humanity require, in the great strife of this world's pride and policy? Alas! who can medicate for soul or body, if the patient will dwell in an unwholesome atmosphere, and eat pernicious food? Before we complain of want of enjoyment or want of efficacy in these sacred mysteries, we must examine ourselves what we do, or mean to do, to counteract their blessed influences.

Those likewise who bring their sorrows to be healed and solaced at the altar; although in

15*

some sense they are the most honest suppliants, for nature loves not sorrow; yet sorrow is a rebellious thing, and often wants the sanctity of submission; and then it is so hard for man to judge in this case between the complaint and the process of its cure. Some secret sin, some indulged corruption, or habit adverse to the mind of God, may have produced the painful dispensation. The physician may know the sorrow is the medicine, not the disease, nor to be intermitted on the first appearance of recovery; the patient knows nothing of all this, and like a sick child, resists the draught, mourns that he is not comforted in prayer, when, if he would only listen he would hear the tender father's most persuasive voice—" My son, depise not thou the chastening of the Lord, nor faint when thou art rebuked of him." Go and examine what it is delays your consolation, that as yet your prayers prevail not to remove his hand; perhaps it will be whispered to you in this study of yourself, Give up that questionable practice, resist that natural propensity, be humbled for that infirmity, or repair that wrong, then will it be safe to close the wound and remove this sorrow from you.

More than all these, perhaps, the wonder seems that they who come to the altar for blessings purely spiritual, for the strengthening of their faith, the increase of their love, and the subjugation of their sins, do so often go away unsatisfied and unassured of benefits received. Most commonly, I believe, this case is one before alluded to; we really have received the things we sought, but have not faith at the time to realise the grant: the excited hope that cheered us to the effort went out, or was put out by the enemy at the altar, and we have come away in mournful unconsciousness of the blessing poured out upon us. If so, let us wait—" The husbandman waiteth for the precious fruit of the earth, and hath long patience for it, until he receive the early and the latter rain;—be ye also patient; stablish your hearts." At the beginning of Daniel's prayer, the commandment came forth, though it was long before it reached the earth. Abraham did not receive the child of promise till it became in the natural course impossible. God does take time for every thing: He took time to make the world, and time to redeem it; and still he takes time to convert and sanctify every separate soul whom he designs for glory. It seems long—" but he that believeth shall not make haste." What is time to one who has all eternity to be blessed in, and only as it were a throb of pain, or breathing of desire, to fill up the brief interval? Hope against hope —believe against experience—believe that ye receive grace and strength, although your hand seems empty and your bosom void. In presence of the enemy, Israel sang the praises of the Lord; and when they began to sing and praise, the enemy was smitten.

But, there is a reverse of this conclusion; there is a possible and too probable forfeiture on our part of even the spiritual benefits intended for us in the Sacrament, by the means we use to counteract them. For why are God's promises of peace and joy so great, and the believer's realisation of them so comparatively little; but because we do not act rationally in furtherance of our best desires? Perhaps while we are earnestly praying for the subjugation of some particular sin, we go needlessly to the scenes most likely to excite it—while we implore strength against the assaults of Satan, we go to meet him where we know his seat is. We ask more faith, and forthwith indulge in conversation or reading calculated to obscure the little that we have. We desire earnestly to grow in grace: and thence proceed to put ourselves under the most unfavorable influences, or deprive ourselves of the most ordinary means. We plant our vines on the cold side of the hill, and wonder that they yield us no rich juices— we scatter our corn upon the common field, and wonder to find it trodden under foot—we leave our fires unstirred and our lamps untrimmed, and complain that we sit in darkness and derive no warmth. This do we—not perhaps in things sinful in themselves, and directly forbidden by the word of God, but in things inexpedient by reason of the influence they have upon our spiritual health, and the divine life within us; especially upon our present enjoyment of it.

Few of us know perhaps what exquisite delight we throw away by this idle tampering with our blessings, and it is the more difficult to know, because no common rules can be laid down that apply to every character alike. What is the harm of this? and what is the use of that? are every-day questions; and there is often no answer to be given but this—the harm is the harm it does us; the use is the good we get by it: either difficult to estimate for another, because the influences are so variable upon different minds. One need not take another's medicine, or observe another's regimen, though all must agree to shun the labelled poisons constantly presented to us in the world; nevertheless, a single eye will gather light enough from experience, to avoid what is injurious and choose what is influentially as well as essentially good; and God vouchsafes to our simplicity the guidance he refuses to our frowardness.

Then let every faithful communicant be aware, that when we leave the Master's table, laden with the rich gifts and treasures of his love, there are watchers at the door to take them from us. The babblers and banterers are there, to make us forget their value, and let them go. The arguers and disputants are there, to offer us some counterfeit in exchange: besides that watchful enemy who waits but an unguarded moment to purloin them. These cannot altogether prevail to snatch us out of our Redeemer's hand; but they can, and they do prevail to snatch his blessings out of ours. But take those blessings home; go privily and cautiously, and count them up and dwell upon them, and pray over them, and store them in the inner chambers of your soul, that you may return to them from your week-day occupations, and find them bright and precious as you received them. The Christian's intensest feelings will scarcely bear the world's unhallowed light. The near communion which the soul sometimes holds with God in Christ, nowhere perhaps nearer than in this communion of his body and blood, is so wordless and incommunicable a thing, that any attempt to give a voice or a name to it, seems to endanger our sense of its reality. It is so near to possession, that it is not hope—so near to sight, that it is scarcely faith. For if we should say at such a time "I believe," it would not be the just expression of our minds. "I see, I know, I feel, the presence, and the power, and the love of my Redeemer-God; I talk with him, I hear him;" these would seem fitter words; but these would not be right ones; because to see, to hear, to speak, are impressions of things external; and seem to put mortal and corporeal senses between the intimacy of spirit with spirit, the nearness of the soul to Him who dwells in it, and in whom

it dwells. Besides that our senses may deceive
us—the sight, the sound, the speech, may be
delusion; it is something far more sure than
these. I believe that, for a brief duration, it is
the very similitude of that state in which the
sister lamps of faith and hope go out, and love
burns on alone. The believer cannot fix this
glimpse of heaven to keep it always visible
through the strife of time. But he can keep the
impression of what he has seen, and call to mind
its proved reality, and dwell upon the time—for
he knows it—when this enjoyment of God shall
be his own for ever. I do not think he can well
submit to earthly gaze this joy, with which a
stranger intermeddleth not. Among Christ's
living members there may be a sign, but for the
most part these are the secret things of a man,
that belong to God.

The near communion which the redeemed
enjoy, when their union with the Redeemer can
be fully realised, being so far incommunicable,
that description would seem inadequate to those
who are sensible partakers of this hidden life;
and to those who are not, can scarcely convey
so much meaning as might persuade them of
enjoyments in religion unattained, and yet within their reach; for the most part I think there is
a better way. The man who has grown rich in
money, does not call his neighbors and friends
together to exhibit his bonds and securities; he
invites them to his table and brings them to his

house, and they perceive by his expenditure, the
change in his condition. Has the Christian no
way but words, to show how rich he is, how
blest he is? When we come from the altar laden
with rich grants of spiritual blessings, comforted,
established, reassured, it should be with us even
as when the face of Moses shone with the bright-
ness of the glory of the holy place. Peace is
too rare a thing in this tumultuous world, to
pass unnoticed; and there is the stamp of heaven so plain upon it, that Satan has been baffled
to devise a counterfeit. And as we do not account that man the most assuredly rich, who
spreads his table profusely, and tricks his house
out gaily, and dresses himself superbly once a
year; but rather him who has the appendages
of affluence always round him; so I think the
believer's possession of God, is not so much
manifested on occasions, by gifts of prayer, and
fervency of discourse, and efforts of self-negation,
and extraordinary acts of faith, however these,
when called for, do manifest the great power of
the Spirit in us to the glory of God. They are
not, I think, so sure an indication of his spiritual
growth, as that habitual plenitude which marks
the abiding of the same Spirit in us—the enjoyment in God of whatever he bestows; the resig-
nation to him of whatever he withdraws; praise
for what we have, and confiding prayer for
what we want, and that freeness and composed-
ness of spirit, which none but the secure and

happy feel, and no sinning dying creature can feel, separate from Christ.

With all our caution to beware that no man take our crown, God's gift of himself is not a miser's treasure, to be buried for safety in the earth. We are to wear it, and to spend it in the sight of all men: "that they, seeing our good works, may glorify our Father which is in heaven." If we be rich in God, it may be seen by the little need we have of other possessions. If we be happy in God, it may be manifested in our daily enjoyment of him, in cheerfulness and contentedness of spirit, without the stimulants of adventitious pleasures. If we be safe in God, it may be seen in the absence of all anxious, carking cares and apprehensions of the time to come. All may be seen in a life of willing obedience to his word, "walking henceforth in his holy ways." Such an expenditure communicates our wealth to all around us, and when men behold it, they will inquire how we came to be so rich; perhaps be persuaded to seek treasure in the Lord.

The ungodly world is ever as Jesus found it: "We have piped unto you, and ye have not danced: we have mourned unto you, and ye have not wept:"—offended at one time by what they call the gloom of religion, its abstinence from forbidden pleasures—they affect at other times to doubt the believer's pretension to a higher happiness, because he seems to enjoy

16

life as much as others;—the delights of nature,
the gifts of Providence, the pursuits of science,
the exercise of our faculties, and the gratification of our tastes and feelings—in short they do
not see that Christians want relish for any thing
that is good. Oh, if they *could* see what lies
beyond their search, they would find it not only
so, but that the Christian is the only one who
tastes the zest of any thing, for God himself is
the zest of all his gifts. The food we eat, the
green turf we tread upon, the fresh breeze that
blows upon our bodies, and invigorates our
limbs, and nature's gay coloring that delights
our eyes—God's universal boon: and those
more special grants, the feasted intellect, [and
satisfied affection, and all that superfluity, that
prodigality of good, with which an indulgent
Father gratifies even the least preferences of
his children: who knows them—who feels them
—who estimates them as the Christian does,
when he enjoys his Maker's [presence in them?
It is the condemnation of the world, that God
is not in all their thoughts; not to detach those
thoughts from any legitimate pursuit, or withhold them from any innocent delight; but God,
the life as well as the source of all, is to be
sought in every pursuit, and enjoyed in every
delight, himself at once the giver and the gift:
as He hereafter shall be all in all, not in the
waste of annihilated being, but in the fulness of
all being, possessed and enjoyed in Him.

r

CHAPTER X.

OF YOUNG PERSONS WHO RECEIVE THE SACRA-
MENT FOR THE FIRST TIME AFTER CONFIR-
MATION.

Our church has determined "that there shall
none be admitted to the Holy Communion,
until such time as he be confirmed, or be ready
and desirous to be confirmed:" a strong refu-
tation, I think, of the arguments drawn from
the wording of some of her formularies, to
prove that the church considers every baptized
child to be really and spiritually regenerate,
and born anew of the Holy Spirit. If this were
to be taken for granted, the so-made child of
God is entitled to be considered a member of
Christ's mystical body, and to be a partaker of his
flesh and blood, without any further examination or evidence of his claims. The determination of the church is otherwise. Dedicated by
the parent's faith and desire, to God, and
pledged to his service in the sponsor's hopes
and prayers, the church receives to her outward privileges, and all the benefit of her instruction and her prayers, the unconscious
infant; assuming as she does throughout her
forms, but not deciding upon, the validity of the

contract between the soul and God—the inward
and spiritual grace signified, but not inherent in
the outward and visible sign. On children so
baptized the church pronounces it " certain by
the word of God, that dying before they commit actual sin, they are undoubtedly saved."
Not, I conceive, because they are baptized, for
that would make the church their Saviour: not
because of their parent's faith, for that would
make a Saviour of the parents, and would besides invalidite the baptism of many, on behalf
of whom no such faith has been exercised; neither, I believe, because the Holy Ghost is then
necessarily received; but because in the view
which the church takes of general redemption,
the one perfect and sufficient satisfaction and
oblation for the sins of the whole world, the
death of Christ, has removed the penalty of
original sin, derived from Adam; the only
charge that could be laid on an unconscious
child, before the age of moral responsibility.
To exhibit this truth, and to confirm it to the
glory of God, and the great consolation of a
parent who loses a child in infancy, I should
consider to be one of the primary objects of
infant baptism. If Jesus takes our dedicated
one before it has been soiled with wilful sin, or
stamped with the guilt of unbelief, he surely
takes his own. If not, whatever the Church
has pronounced, on the assumption that the
outward profession has been accompanied by

the inward and spiritual grace, she attaches no
such certainty of acceptance with God, as would
entitle the baptised to the more exclusive ceremony of the Lord's Supper, reserved and
restricted to the faithfnl, to them that actually,
not ceremonially, and by the faith of another,
do truly repent them of their sins, and believe
the promises of God in Jesus Christ. If, in
stating my own views, I misrepresent those of
the church, I do so without design; but I think
this interposition of the rite of confirmation
between the baptism in which the child is
assumed to be made a child of God, and the
communion of the Lord's Supper, in which he
is accepted as such, is a strong testimony that
the church does not decide upon the efficacy of
the first administration. Like many worldly
contracts, which, however solemn and binding
on the conscience, and however confidently
relied upon, can have no legal validity, till the
contracting party is of age; the solemnly-taken
covenant of baptism; waits the signature of the
matured and instructed proselyte, before it is
received in evidence of a Christian profession.
The pious parent's hopes, meantime, are in
abeyance, upheld by a far surer ground of confidence than this incomplete transaction, the
faithful promise of God, of a divine blessing
upon their instruction, their example, and their
prayers; till the child having incurred the penalty of actual and personal transgression, is

16*

capable by faith, and repentance, and application of the blood of Christ, to ratify and perform his part of the contract; as by devoting and bringing him up to God, the parents have alredy performed theirs.

To this intent the rite of confirmation has been established: a brief and beautiful service, which supposes the previous examination of every candidate and satisfaction received, as far as profession can give it, that he is indeed born anew of the Spirit, and a living member of the body of Christ, meet to sit down at the table of the faithful. Such examination made and attested by those who ought to be most competent to judge—as the leper of old was admitted to the congregation when by certain divinely-ordained tests the priests pronounced him clean— so the church does again, as we have observed her to do throughout, accept the profession of which God alone can judge; and with the onlaid hand of blessing, pronounces their souls regenerate and their sins forgiven; prays for a continuance of the grace and increase of the divine life assumed to be received; and can at no time after, I believe, except by occasion of gross and outward transgression, refuse the communion, or claim to re-examine the communicant. Impressed as I am with the excellent wisdom and fitness of this whole arrangement, I cannot but be impressed also with the careless and inadequate manner with which the purpose of the church has come to be executed. Whether from the persuasion that the actual assumption of the Christian profession takes place in baptism, without the consent or knowledge of the professor, and contrary to all subsequent experience, or from the belief that it cannot be verified by any form at all, confirmation has come to be treated very lightly, as something indifferent, to be done or let alone. To me, I confess, the letting alone seems less objectionable than the so doing: for the church itself does not consider the *act* indispensable, provided the person is ready and desirous to perform it, should occasion serve: whereas in the actual performance as usually effected, there is neither readiness nor desire: the parent performs the baptismal proxy over again, directs the child when to be confirmed; and with some better understanding, perhaps, of the nature of the engagement, it remains just as little voluntary as it was before. I fear I may cross the opinions of the pious, as well as the practice of the careless, in expressing my views upon this subject; but considering confirmation as in a manner the completion of the baptismal ceremony, I think it ought in nowise to be performed, until the young person is seriously determined to take upon himself the baptismal engagement, and enter into covenant with God in Jesus Christ: until they are believed to have, and believe themselves to have, not by their

sureties but in themselves, what is required of
them that come to be baptised—" Repentance,
whereby they forsake sin; and faith, whereby
they stedfastly believe the promises of God
made to them in that sacrament." The case is
not now what it was before: the church can no
longer assume that the baptised child may die;
and without repentance for the sin it has been
incapable of committing, or faith in Him whom
it has been incapable of knowing, be admitted
to the benefits of a free salvation. The candidate for confirmation appears in the visible
likeness of the fallen Adam, the possessed inheritor of Adam's sin—in a position, therefore,
in which, without faith and repentance, he has
no right to suppose himself, or be by us supposed, the subject of salvation; nor can be called
upon to assert it on the authority of others:
still less be pronounced by faith and hope
an elect-member of the church of Christ: his
calling and election can only now be made
sure by the manifestation of divine life within.
Before the infant eye is capable of distinguishing
objects or indicating its notice of them, the mo-
ther believes and hopes her babe will have its
eye-sight; but the time comes when she can only
know it by the manifest exercise of the visual
powers. So in the spiritual life of her offspring,
she may hope and believe, and if her babe dies
be assured of it—" For of such is the kingdom
of heaven." If it lives, in faith she may still en-

joy the substance of things hoped-for, the evidence of things not seen: she may believe that God will at some time manifest his blessing on her care, and his acceptance of her prayers, by imparting his life-giving Spirit to her child. Most firmly I believe he will do so—not because He has said—" Whosoever is baptised shall be saved;"—for He has never said it;—but because he has said, " Bring up a child in the way that it should go, and when it is old it will not depart from it." But to persist in thinking that her offspring *has been* so made alive, and teaching it so to believe, when not a symptom of spiritual vitality appears, is to my mind, on the part of the parent a most awful presumption, and to the child a most ruinous delusion: making of none effect or value the whole testimony of Scripture, which requires that the tree be known by its fruit, and admits no testimony of of a justified state, but the work of the Holy Spirit in the heart.

While the child is yet uninstructed and irresponsible, it is the parent, not the child, that fulfils the baptismal engagement—fulfils on its behalf what on its behalf they have undertaken; by allowing nothing that is contrary to the vow, and enforcing such habits, and instilling such precepts as are in exact conformity with it. As the child becomes capable of understanding the will of God, and the method of salvation, its own duties and responsibilities are unfolded and en-

forced; not because it has made an engagement
to that effect, which the child will very early
discover to be a fiction, but because it is a divine
and universal obligation to believe and obey the
Gospel. As long and to the extent that the
young person's actions continue to be under pa-
rental control, I think the parents continue bound
by the utmost extent of the vow—not because
the child has taken it, but because they have.—
If I tell my daughter that I cannot indulge her
in worldly pomps and pleasures, because *she*
has promised to renounce them, it is no argument, and she perceives the fallacy: she knows
she has not done so, and perhaps is not determined that she ever will. If I tell her on the contrary that these things are contrary to my own
profession as a child of God, and to my engagement to bring her up in the paths of godliness,
and therefore, cannot be consented to whilst I
have the right to control her actions, she is competent to appreciate the argument, as founded
on truth and candor.

How early young people are capable of taking
the engagement upon themselves, and volunta-
rily entering upon a life of faith, I feel it impossible to decide. The seeds of divine life sometimes spring up so very early, that the age at
which it is possible for a child to be ready and
desirous to be confirmed, cannot be taken for
that at which it may commonly be expected.   I
do not wish to prescribe an age; but I should

think generally that confirmation in our church takes place too soon. I confine this observation to our own church, because I am not informed at what age the Presbyterian and dissenting churches examine their young people preparatory to their admission to the communion. I take it for granted that some such public profession is required in every Christian community; and whatever it be that stands in the place of our act of confirmation, I consider it in the same light: it is not the form that signifies, it is the intention; it is that, whatever it be, by which, as far as human insight can, the communion is guarded from the intrusion of the unconverted. I can only say for myself, that whatever be the practice of our own or other communities, I could not, as a parent, a guardian, or a sponsor, bring a child to be confirmed till it manifested a voluntary, well-considered, and well-instructed desire, to confess the faith of Christ crucified, and to fight under his banner against the world, the flesh, and the devil, and to continue Christ's faithful soldier and servant unto his life's end: or whatever form of profession to the same effect any church communion may prescribe.

The form of confirmation is very simple and very explicit; and with the same tenderness for the weak and ill-assured that pervades our whole ritual, the demand upon the candidate is so very moderate, that it need not falter the most timid and conscientious replicant, provided he be indeed of the miud to take these vows upon him.' Nothing is asked of what has heretofore been done—nothing is said of broken vows and baptismal promises unkept. I must again remark, that the candidate for confirmation is not addressed on his actual adoption into the family of God, reminded of his previous responsibility as a child of God, or confessed or prayed for as a transgressor of a covenant, assumed to have been made by him in baptism; all which I should have expected, had the church taken the view of that Sacrament which some persons inculcate. "Children being come to years of discretion," and fully instructed in all the Christian faith, " having learned what their godfathers and godmothers promised for them in baptism," and being supposed to understand the nature of repentance, whereby they forsake sin, and faith whereby they receive the promises of God made to them in that Sacrament, are called upon to say before God and that congregation, whether they will ratify and confirm the engagements made for them, and do consider themselves bound to believe and to do the things therein specified, and will by the grace of God endeavor faithfully to observe tnem. On the part of the young proselyte, the ceremony ends with this: the remainder of the performance is the prayer of the church on their behalf, and her assurance, not theirs, that in so confessing their obligation and desiring to fulfil it, they are influenced by

the Holy Spirit, accepted of the Father, and received into the faith of Christ. The category
proceeds no farther; the pledge is taken for no
more; the young confessor is not called upon to
say that he has repented and believed; has
washed himself in the fountain opened for sin
and for uncleanness, or received forgiveness of
his sins, and the earnest of the Spirit in his soul.
This would be too much to say, because on their
young experience and indistinct self-knowledge,
it is more than they can generally know. Self-
knowledge is the acquisition of maturer years—
the latest growth of intellect and the autumn
fruit of grace. In very young persons whom
God prepares for an early removal to glory, the
most perfect and vivid experience and enjoyment of the life in Christ is sometimes manifested, a realised hope so unmixed and unpertur-
bed, that one might fancy the great enemy had
seen them cradled from their birth in the pa-
noply of heaven, and never ventured to lay his
hand upon them. But these are not creatures
of the earth, or long to remain upon it. Generally, so far from soliciting, I could scarcely
welcome in young people a precocious confidence of their own calling and election in Jesus
Christ. I should think *hope* a better blossom
than *assurance*, and *desire* a safer evidence than
experience. Not because the youngest, even
the infant member of Christ is less safely and
eternally united to him than the most matured

17

saint; but because it is a time when feelings
are so liable to take the form of principles, and
the perceptions have so much the advance of
the understanding, the most artless mind is
only the most exposed to self-deception. Again,
therefore, I would bear testimony to the wisdom and moderation of the church in requiring
no profession or promise, from the candidate for
confirmation, but such as at the appointed age
instructed youth is fully competent to make:
namely, whether they consider themselves
bound to do and believe the things in which
they have been instructed, and by the grace of
God will evermore endeavor faithfully to observe that, which by their own mouth and consent they acknowledge that they ought to do:
the first developement of living faith—assent to
the truth of the Gospel, and determination to
obey it. This profession solemnly and publicly
made, and every means used on the part of the
minister and other spiritual instructors to ascer-
tain its sincerity, the church admits the confessor
to the exclusive privilege of the faithful—the
most holy communion of the body and blood of
our Saviour Christ: and it is generally expected
that they should appear at the table on the
earliest opportunity subsequent to confirmation.
All is thus done that can be done by others:
and most deep, and serious, and entire becomes
now the responsibility of the young Christian—
"To examine themselves whether they repent

them truly of their former sins, stedfastly purposing to lead a new life; have a lively faith in
God's mercy through Christ, with a thankful
remembrance of his death, and are in love and
charity with all men."

"I am the true vine," says the Lord, "and
my Father is the husbandman. Every branch
in me that beareth not fruit he taketh away:
and every branch in me that beareth fruit, he
purgeth it that it may bring forth more fruit."
In vain the church's blessing and assurance, the
sponsor's faith and parent's anxious cares; in
vain the water sprinkled, the precious emblems
taken and received; if this engrafted bud become not a living, growing and fruit-bearing
branch of that life-giving, life-sustaining stem.
True, the Father is a patient husbandman.
He does not look to gather of his vintage in the
spring time, or cull his grapes before the flower
is set: but He is skilful too, and knows the
first germinating promise of the future fruit,
and sees if it is not there. We need not fear
to carry the figure on, for it is his own chosen
imagery, exhibiting by things familiar to the
simplest and the youngest, the most mysterious
secrets of his truth. Have we not seen the
carefully-tended plant, trained and watered and
cultured day by day; and watched some branch
of it that never buds: that keeps its wintry
aspect all the year: and though to sight
attached to the vigorous root, it draws no nour-

ishment from it, and puts forth no leaves to
grace it, and remains an ugly and distorted
thing, only to disfigure the fair plant. And
have we not seen other off-sets of a sickly
growth—full of leaves, and useless wild lux-
uriance, pretty in spring, but an incumbrance
as the time of fruit approaches, of which it
gives no promise. Attached are these also to
the source of life and nourishment, and have
derived some measure of succor from it; but
nothing of its fruit-producing life and vigor.
Yes, and we know what comes of them—what
must come of them, when the pruner's knife
approaches: they must not stay to shame the
culture and to spoil the tree. God is indeed a
patient husbandman: he does not his work as
men do: He comes round many and many a
year, and watches these young scions of his
confessing church, to see if they be indeed its
believing, repenting and obedient members.
And why so often? " He knows them that are
his"—and did know from all eternity who they
were; but this is not the way he works. He
suffers them to be engrafted—he allows them
to remain—he lets them take and renew their
baptismal vows—lets them come month by
month and sit among the faithful at his feast.
He does much more than this: for meantime
his rains descend and his dews to water the
earth, and many a summer's sun shines out
upon these branches. He pours into the

young ear the persuasions of his love, and exhibits before their eyes the warnings of his anger. He compasses them, as it were, with an atmosphere of grace, in the prayers and preaching and ordinances of the church, into which they have been received. And then he waits—O how long he waits!

The most lifeless, the most graceless communicant may gaze upon the emblems of redeeming love, and when he hears it said, " Which was shed *for you,*"—" which was broken *for you,*"—may be assured that to that body and blood he owes the suspensive mercy that [gives him time to repent and believe, to bring forth fruits meet for repentance, and to work the work of faith. But, " if a man abide not in me, he is cast forth as a branch, and is withered; and men gather them up and cast them into the fire, and they are burned." The pruning time must come. And ˋhere let the young ones pause; and let the new proselytes listen; and whether they be going to the sacrament unprepared, or have determined to remain unprepared away, let them deeply consider their position. He who has a sum of money in possession, knows by his expenditure how much there is remaining; the simple peasant who notches days upon a stick, and cuts off the notches as another and another passes, can reckon how many he has left. But to you, the fewer gone are no imitation of the more

17*

to come; the small expenditure no proof of
wealth remaining; brief as the time may be,
and few as the years may be that have been
lost in godlessness and folly, you may not
have as many remaining to redeem them.
The off-casting of the worthless branch waits
no fixed season; it must be when the health
and beauty of the tree require it, and the
wisdom of the husbandman so determines;
perhaps when the unholy influence and example would become injurious to others; when
the false profession or inconsistent life would
bring disgrace upon religion, and shame the
name of Christ. And this is not all. There
are other risks than the uncertainty of life, and
other dangers than untimely death. We know
that the sudden tempest lays low the diseased
and rotten tree, and scatters the dead branches
on the ground, while it leaves uninjured and
unmoved the firm and thriving ones. But have
we not seen also when the long winter snows
begin to melt, when the iron-hearted frost gives
way, and we go round our borders to see what
mischief has been done? We know which it
is that we most surely miss. It is not those
that had taken deep root and made a vigorous
growth, before the winter came; they lift their
scatheless heads to the returning sunshine, and
seem to triumph in the desolation; the ruined
ones are those that had a sickly and redundant
growth, that were imperfectly rooted, attached

too feebly to the parent plant, or otherwise ill prepared to bide the blighting time. Yes; and I have seen the same amid the trials and sorrows of the world. The very affliction which has brought light and life into the penitent soul, strengthened the faith, and confirmed the hope, and purified the character of the believer, making Christ thrice precious to him, and himself more like to Christ; I have seen the same affliction chill to death the fictitious excitements of religious feeling, the feeble stirrings of an awakened conscience. I have seen it turn the natural heart to stone, instead of breaking it into godly sorrow; and together with the withered sympathies and blighted promise of young, untried existence, indifference has laid its icy hand upon the early yearnings of the soul towards God. I have observed it often in the poor and in the rich, and watched the declension of what seemed a religious disposition, under the growing pressure of adversity, till the rootless promise has utterly died away. The closed Bible, the neglected church, the avoided counsellers—how well we know the first symptoms of revolt and disavowal; no leisure, no spirits, no resolution now to go with them that keep holiday before the Lord. And then there follows, with the poor, the neglected person, the slovenly house, the domestic discord, dissolute habits, and disaffection to the laws. With the rich, habits of dissipation,

frivolity, and selfishness, to get rid of the
poignancy of remaining feeling, or fill the
void of sympathies extinguished. All this I
have seen to grow out of unsanctified affliction,
and disappointed earthliness; out of those very
trials, which, acting upon a living faith, are the
culture with which the watchful husbandman
purges the branches that they may bring forth
more fruit. They used to hear the gospel;
they used to come to the sacrament; they used
to pray in their families, and keep strict the
Sabbath. What has happened? Oh, the
blighting time has come, and they have
withered away, because they had no root. And
if the winter had spared them, there had come
the drought and heats of summer. Prosperity
is thought to be more dangerous than adversity; and so it is, in so far that while adversity
pursues us, it may be hoped it is the pruner's
knife to purify and invigorate the branches:
whereas unsanctified prosperity is the known
wages of the wicked one; but if that hope
prove fallacious, I know not whether prosperity
or adversity has the more hardening influence
on the heart of the impenitent; if the happy
forget God, the miserable defy him. Oh could
the young disciple but be persuaded what he
risks by hesitating, how soon the soft emotions
of his soul may die away; how-soon the sacred
influences and opportunities may be withdrawn;
how the touching incidents of Jesus' dying love

will become stale and wearisome as an oft-told tale; till they listen with indifference, or listen not at all, to the entreaties of the blessed Lord, who waits even now without, while they delay to open. Then if it should be, as it may not be, that they live out the common term of life, it will be only to fill up the measure of their sin, and the vial of wrath to be poured out upon them. "Now is the accepted time, now is the day of salvation." "All things are ready, come ye to the supper." There never can be a time when all is so ready, so suitable, so inviting. The church has taught you, prayed for you, blessed you, expects you. Your understanding has been enlightened, and your heart affected, and your conscience moved, to acknowledge the claims of God upon you, and all the workings of his mercy towards you. And He —if there can be supposed a time when the gift of a heart is more acceptable to him than at any other, it is, it must be before that heart is seventimes dyed with habits of corruption; is used and worn, and indurated in a baser service.

Yes, if there is a time above every time when Jesus is ready, it is now. Go up to his feast— Go while your heart is warm, and your impressions fresh, and your desires strong. Do not wait to be sure you shall not change your mind, shall not break your vows, and so incur the threatened condemnation. If you give not yourself to Christ, and keep not your mind to

follow him, you are perjured already, and condemned already; for you have taken upon you
the most solemn obligation so to do. Go as
you are—go with what you have—take your
untried affections, your vacillating desires, your
scarcely formed resolutions—lay them upon his
altar, and tell him it is all you have. Remember the two mites that only made a farthing—
but she had no more, and so they were enough.
You know not yet how little that blessed master will accept from those who do what they
can:—how small the grain of mustard-seed is
which he acknowledges, and blesses the future
germ of faith; and sets himself, loving and
tender and most faithful husbandman, to nurture, and cherish, and protect the feeble thing;
nay, does become himself its life, indissoluble,
indestructible, eternal. Go up, and say to him
that you do not know if it be so with you or
not, but that you wish it were: you are not
sure if you will give yourself to him, but you
wish that he would take you. Entreat him to
it by his body and blood that will be exhibited
before you in a figure; by his cross and passion
that you will celebrate; by the anguish of his
soul on that last evening; by the sympathies of
his manhood at that last supper; by the power
of his godhead now upon the throne, beseech
him, and beseech the Father through him, and
for these things' sake; and beseech him to beseech the Father too, that you go not empty

away, that you return not as ignorant, as unde-
cided, as uncertain of your own disposition as
you came: that you may know indeed, and feel
indeed, and manifest before all men, the growing, acting, fructifying vitality of that faith, into
which you were baptized, and by your own
choice professed. If he hear you, and when did
he not hear, though it was but a believing sigh,
I cannot tell you what you will have gained.
It was easy to tell you what you risked, by de-
laying to devote yourself to God; but I cannot
—for I have not learned it all, and what I know,
I have not language to communicate—I cannot
tell you all that you will gain by this early devotion of yourself to God, and immediate entrance on the path of life. Some sacrifices, it is
true, there are to make, but they are far less
now, than they will be by and by.   It is not so
hard to leave a stranger, whom we have but
just now made acquaintance with, as a long
familiar, fascinating friend.   You know it is not
so hard to leave a place, however charming,
where you have passed but a single night, as
one in which you have made yourself a home,
and become attached to every thing around you.
If any body tells you that by becoming religious,
and separating from the world when young, you
make a greater sacrifice, and relinquish a greater
enjoyment than if you partake of its pleasures
till you are tired, and give yourself to God when
the delights of youth and novelty are over, they

tell you falsely. The world has pleasures—for the worldly: sin has pleasures—for the sinful: but neither sin nor the world has any pleasures for the godly. Youth and a religious education may have prevented you hitherto from being, in respect of habit, either worldly or sinful; and if you renounce them now, those fictitious pleasures will have no charm or attraction in your future life. Intoxication has its pleasures, as is sufficiently proved by the difficulty which is found in relinquishing it after frequent indulgence, and the ruin which men knowingly incur for the enjoyment of it. But do you think the youth who turns with disgust from the taste of spirits, loses an opportunity of enjoyment through his ignorance? O no—you do not think so— and if you should see a young brother preparing to take the first spirituous draught, you would dash it from his lips, lest he should learn to love it. You may go into the world—we would not deceive you, and if you take your unregenerate nature with you, for every guilty pleasure that you find without, you will find a guilty taste within, and for every vanity a vain desire, and for every forbidden object a forbidden wish, and for every hurtful thing a hurtful lust: and they will all grow stronger on the food that suits them, and more importunate to renew the feast; till what is at first the zest of novelty, will presently become the necessity of habit. Then, if by the grace of God, in recollection of your first

impressions, you return again to the point at
which you now hesitate, and resolve to take up
the profession of godliness you now refuse,.
mundane affections will so have wound their
tortuous folds about you, there will be some tie
to break, some sympathy to forego, some interest
to sacrifice at every step—perhaps to pour a bitter into the sweetest offices of love, and bring
even duty and conscience into perpetual collision;
all which might have been avoided, had you
formed your early associations where they will
grow on to eternity, under the blessing of the
Most High. Yea—fly them as you will, and
make what sacrifices you can, there are those
among your first associations that will come after
you, pursue you to the sanctuary, kneel by you
at the altar, shame you by their base companion-
ship in presence of your Lord, and mingle pollution with your purest joys. Be sure the images
of by-gone sins will come; unholy thoughts, in-
veterate habits, incautious language; not a day
will pass, but the pure Spirit within you will be
grieved, and your own peace disturbed, by the
forcible entry of these sometime-encouraged in-
mates of your bosom, till you cry out as St. Paul
did, under a similar conflict, "O wretched man
that I am, who shall deliver me from the body
of this death!" Thanks be to God through
Jesus Christ, it can be done, and by his most
gracious undertaking is done—but how much
more pleasing is the task to him, how much less

18

painful, and wearisome, and discouraging to the soul itself, before habit and indulgence have nursed into activity every indwelling sin; before the strong man armed has fortified his house by engaging every sentiment and taste and feeling on his side!

But however pleasurable sin and folly are to the sinner and the fool, because they are the aliments suited to his nature, not so pleasurable, nor so suitable are they to him, as are the ways of godliness to the child of God. He who invites you into the family of his adopted, has an entertainment prepared for you suited to your new character, to the new man you are exhorted to put on. He does not bid you sacrifice this life to the next; He offers you the life that now is as well as that which is to come; sweets that will leave no bitterness upon the lip: joys that will instruct you of the joys of heaven—blessings that will prepare you for eternal blessedness. Happy indeed, if you will taste and see that he is gracious, before your appetite is utterly vitiated by longer feeding upon time and sense.

We exhort you, then, to go—to go now to the Lord's table: not presumptuously, not inconsiderately, not because you were baptized before you knew good or evil, or because you have recently been brought to the Bishop to be confirmed: but because you desire in your heart to be accepted of him as a member of Christ, a child of God, and an inheritor of the kingdom of heaven; with all the distinctive characters that separate such a one from a world that lieth in wickedness, the children of the wicked one; because you desire, renouncing the pomps and vanities of the world, and the sinful lusts of the flesh, to put on the wedding garment prepared for you; to put on the Lord Jesus Christ—the robe of righteousness, the garment of salvation. We do not tell you first "to make your calling and election sure." You are called now—Jesus has sent for you—the church has fetched you— "the Spirit and the bride say, Come; and let him that heareth say, Come; and let him that is athirst come." We say to you "Choose ye this day whom ye will serve." If there be in you but a considerate choice, an honest desire, it came from God; it is his own good seed; when you present it to him He will know his own, and for his own sake will accept both it and you.

MEDITATIONS AND PRAYERS.

18*

MEDITATIONS AND PRAYERS.

MEDITATIONS ON THE LORD'S PRAYER PREPARATORY TO THE COMMUNION.

" AFTER THIS MANNER PRAY YE."—Matt. vi, 9.

PRAYER has been called the breath of spiritual life; by its free and healthful exercise the vigor of the soul is both sustained and manifested: and by its cessation, that life would be at the least suspended and become insensible. To Him who penetrates beyond the words, if He needed such a disclosure, the tone of our prayers would exactly make known the condition of our hearts; and needless, to Him, they may be most useful to disclose it to ourselves. The church therefore has required, that before we be admitted to the communion, we be able to repeat the Lord's Prayer: a very small and simple requisition, as before men, who can but hear the words; but in its full bearing before Him who searches the heart and taught us so to express ourselves, it contains the full realisa- ·tion of the Gospel faith: and verily and indeed repeated, with an understanding mind, a consenting will, and a beseeching heart, it contains all that is necessary to test our fitness for the holy communion of the body and blood of Christ.

The question then comes home to me: am I able to repeat the Lord's prayer? "After this manner pray ye." The words are so very few, and so very simple, it would seem no very difficult thing, after this example, to frame acceptable prayer. It might be thought to discountenance the efforts that are made for long continuance of attention, and great fervency of expression in the out-pouring of our souls to God; but certainly presents no discouragement to the slow of heart and slow of speech, whose brief, and broken, and almost worldless prayers are their frequent grief and disquietude. The Lord's Prayer is a perfect contrast to all that we call fluency, the excited feeling, the exuberant vehemence, and multiplied invocations which usually characterise all human compositions; yet, besides that, it is, as it must be, the most perfect example of acceptable and accepted service. What Christian suppliant but has sometime felt, after continued efforts to pray, or prolonged attention to the prayers of others, the force and power and sufficiency with which these words have come to our relief, and said for us in a few brief sentences, all that we have been vainly endeavoring to express. Many are the times we can recal, when after an hour, or half an hour's saying, or reading of prayers, we only began to pray when we came to this conclusion, "Who has taught and commanded us thus to pray."

"After this manner." I apprehend the intention of our Lord was not so much to leave us a prayer, as an example of prayer; a pattern by which to frame and methodize those supplications which our various situations, feelings, and necessities would suggest. Few words and few desires; calm, direct, concentrated; the state of our hearts betrayed in our desires; faith rather exercised than professed; obedience rather asked than promised; much meant, and little told, and nothing argued. Oh how simply and confidently, in this brief interview with the Father, the soul seems, as it were, to give itself up, and throw its whole concernment upon God.

Can I then repeat the Lord's Prayer? If I can, I may fearlessly approach the table prepared by Jesus for the brethren of his Father's household, for whom it was intended, and to whom alone adapted. I need not be deterred or distressed, because my heart does not understand its own emotions, cannot explain its own necessities, or connect its wishes, or prolong its intercessions. What I call my worst prayers— hasty, disjointed, interrupted—are more like

this, perhaps, than some that I am better
pleased with. Peter said little when he was
afraid of sinking; when he wept bitterly at the
denial of his master, he probabiy said nothing:
and few prayers were briefer than *his*, who it
is probable never said but one, and asked all,
and received all in that 'single grant—" Lord,
remember me." No supplications, perhaps, are
so powerful with God, so true, so real, as those
which in a beating, breaking heart, the Holy
Spirit makes, with groanings that cannot be
uttered; that heart scarce knowing if it prays
or not, but only that it would pray if it could,
and must break if it be not heard.

PRAYER.

Almighty God, who hast given us words,
which without thy Spirit we cannot use, enable
me, I beseech thee, so to examine myself by
them, that I come not with vain babbling before
thee, without feeling, without understanding, to
judge myself, and eat and drink my own condemnation. Suffer not the enemy to blind my eyes
with false emotions, and vain resolutions, and
fictitious hopes, to hide from me the real condition of my soul. Before I presume to eat of thy
bread, and drink of thy cup, and call myself by
thy name, and take thy sacred words upon my.
lips, O merciful God, grant me thy light to know

what I am saying, and faith to believe it, and grace to pursue it, in the Spirit of Him, who taught me thus to pray. Amen.

" OUR FATHER WHICH ART IN HEAVEN."

"Our Father." The Father of our Lord Jesus Christ, who is said to be the first-born of many brethren—" My Father and your Father." The family of God, the children of the Most High, and brethren of Jesus Christ, are not the world entire. " Wherefore come out from among them, and be ye separate, saith the Lord, and touch not the unclean thing; and I will be a Father unto you, and ye shall be my sons and daughters, saith the Lord Almighty." And forasmuch as of him the whole family in heaven and earth are named, they are those exclusively who bear the name of Christ, and walk in his Spirit. "For as many as are led by the Spirit of God they are the sons of God." As many and no more: not all the thousands who from their infancy repeat this prayer, nor even the hundreds who at every celebration, "sit as my people sitteth," at his holy table. The Creator and Sovereign Lord of all men, has never called himself the Father of the fallen world: nor answers to that appellation, until he has first sent forth the Spirit of his Son into our hearts, " crying, Abba, Father." Then, ere I present my petition to the King of Kings, am I right in the superscription, in which every name and attribute of Deity is put aside; and lest the cry of the servant should intermingle as it were, and overbear the confidence of the child, the Abba stands alone. This prayer which I thought so easy and have said so often, I now almost hesitate to begin, lest I mix with that sweet sound the voice of fear, or cry of unwilling subjugation.— "If I be a father, where is my honor," saith the Almighty. "If God were your Father, ye would love me," said the blessed Jesus. The first sentence of the Lord's prayer is a confession of the Christian faith, full and explicit as any length of words could make it, in which I profess to believe myself a child of God, a member of Christ, and an inheritor of the kingdom of Heaven. Is it true? Let no one deceive himself, and venture with this address to approach the throne on which the God of nature sits alone, his majesty untempered by the sweet incense of the atoning sacrifice. "He that hath not the Son hath not the Father;" hath no such father, and if I begin my prayer without this meaning, without the faith of Christ and the influence of the Spirit, I give it to the winds, for there is none to own it. In one sense, the highest and most precious sense in which we are privileged thus to address our Maker, God has properly speaking but one Son, " This is my beloved Son, in whom I am well pleased:" The only-begotten

2ry say

of the Father, in whom, as members united to one head, we are brought into that near relationship to God which he so graciously acknowledges, and so mysteriously calls "fellowship:" "Fellowship with God the Father, and with the Son."

I cannot compass that mystery, but I can enjoy its blessedness; I know not the manner of the union, but I can taste the sweetness of this near communion with Him. If I know no more, I know what a Father is. God has a great incommunicable name; but he does not call himself by that. He has a covenant name, Jehovah, mighty to save! but it is not by that he teaches us to call him. I know not why, in the prayer of his own inditing, this single appellation stands alone, except it be because he loves it best, and best delights in the spirit that can use it, and the state of mind that it expresses; and if it be so, I cannot better prepare to present myself acceptably before him, than by imbibing of this spirit, the spirit of adoption, the feelings of a child, simple, submissive, and confiding; pleased to depend on him, willing to be ruled by him, earnest to please him, and sure to be beloved of him.

PRAYER.

O Thou, who of thy great love hast called thyself our Father, and chosen to thyself a

family in Jesus Christ, put thou upon me, I beseech thee, the seal of thine adoption, the name
and image of thy own blessed Son, that I
may come with holy confidence before thee,
and take without fear the blessings of thy
house. And grant that feeding in faith upon
the body and blood of Christ, I may be assured
of my eternal union with him, in whom thou
art well-pleased; and be admitted to more near
communion with thee, in the sensible fellowship of thy Holy Spirit. O God, if it be thy
pleasure this day to receive me as thy child, put
from me the spirit of bondage and the sinful
habits of the world, that being enabled neither
to dishonor nor distrust thee, I may walk before
men in righteousness and peace, and enter now
into the rest prepared for thy family on earth
and in heaven, here and for ever. Amen.

"HALLOWED BE THY NAME."

Alas! how often has the lying lip profaned
that name, in the very utterance of this false
petition! Where was I last night? Where do
I mean to be to-morrow? What did I last before I came to say the prayer? What shall I do
next, as soon as it is over? It is by the suppliant himself, very often, God sends the acceptance or rejection of the petition: and I may be
the first to join in some unhallowed jest, or some

ungodly sport; to break the sanctity of the Sabbath, or take his name in vain: or contrariwise, to vindicate the Father's honor and approve my prayer, by a refusal to countenance or mix with those that do so. Did I say rejection? This is a prayer that never was rejected: but the heart that means to sin or loves to sin, can be heard in it only to condemnation; when although we mean it not, and wish it not, God's holiness will be vindicated, and his name be sanctified in the destruction of the wicked: of thousands who so pray but do not so intend. Oh, why am I afraid to go to the Sacrament only with an impenitent heart, lest I provoke God's judgments against me—I do in this very prayer invoke them. I implore his sanctifying spirit upon all who profess his name, that they may glorify him; his judgments upon all who dishonor and despise it, that He may glorify himself. By his grace in me, or by his wrath upon me, his name must finally be hallowed, and my prayer fulfilled; and every time I repeat it, I pronounce him just when He judges, and clear when He condemns. In this again is the faith of Christ exhibited—is is the disciple's prayer—it is Christian character added to Christian principle: works added to our faith. "He that dishonoreth me, dishonoreth the Father that sent me." It is God's name in Christ, and Christ's name in me, that I desire may be hallowed: for inasmuch as we have taken his holy name upon us, and are become his sanctuary upon earth, " we are the temples of the living God;" whatever brings disgrace upon our profession, or puts us to deserved shame; or unseen of men, affords a triumph to the powers of darkness, does indeed unhallow the name of Christ, and in him of the Father. " If any man defile the temple of God, him shall God destroy;—which temple are ye." Should I multiply words without number, I could not express more strongly my desire and purpose to lead a godly and religious life. " Hallowed be thy name"—the name of Christ, the name of Christian. How have the pure characters of that new name been exhibited hitherto in this perturbed and guilty bosom? If from the heart, in all its recesses, we can breathe this wish, little could be added in condemnation of our sins past, and aspirations after holiness in our lives to come. For who has dishonored my Father's name as I have: or who, unless he hear me in this suit, so likely, nay, so sure, to dishonor it again? Can I proceed with a prayer that condemns me, and utter aspirations after holiness that my sinful heart may presently deny, my lips and conversation seem to contradict? Yes—for I come to ask, and not to promise. " Blessed are they that hunger and thirst after righteousness, for they shall be filled." In the deep hatred of my soul for sin, in its intensest longings after holiness, in bitterest remembrance of the times when I have

uttered this name, without thought, heard it
without emotion, dishonored it without remorse,
I can use this prayer, for he knows that to will
is present with me; and when to perform I find
not, I will still repeat it, until he arise and help
me for his great name sake.

PRAYER.

Hear thou my prayer, O God, in mercy, not
in judgment, and for thy great name's sake take
away the transgressions with which I have dishonored and profaned it, that they be no more
found. So cleanse me with the blood of Christ
that I may be worthy to bear his name;
and forasmuch as I go now to thy altar to
profess myself his disciple, give me courage, O
gracious Lord, hereafter to confess him before
all men, and live to the honor and glory of his
name, in an ungodly and unbelieving world.
Prevent me, I beseech thee, this day, that I
profane not thy holy mysteries, with levity and
carelessness—with vain and worldly thoughts—
that I bring not any idols in my heart, to unhallow thy sanctuary and mock thy sacred rite.
Above all, Lord Jesus, prevent me, that I give
not to these thy creatures the worship and the
power that belongs only to thee, blessed Saviour, one and very God, in whom only is salvation. Amen.

19*

" THY KINGDOM COME."

This prayer is addressed to God the Father.
It is, therefore, the kingdom of the Father that
is intended: as it is variously called in Scripture, the kingdom of God—the kingdom of
heaven. But it is also written that the Father
hath committed all government to the Son—all
power in heaven and earth. " The government shall be upon his shoulder, and he shall
be called Wonderful, Counsellor, the everlasting
Father." Christ in his kingly character assumes his Father's name—sits down upon his
throne—receives the kingdom from him. And
thus, it is the kingdom of Christ that is invoked,
although the Father only is addressed. Many
have been surprised that there is no mention of
Christ in this prayer: and it is possible that
some have even ventured to use it in unbelief
of Christ: whereas, he is indeed the life and
unction of the whole, without whom it has no
meaning, as it can have no acceptance: for as
we have already seen that there is no Father of
a fallen world, except the Father of our Lord
Jesus Christ, so neither is there any kingdom
of God into which a sinner can enter, but the
kingdom of Christ the anointed of the Father.
Unless we mean this, we mean nothing. And
alas! very many do mean nothing when they
go on from day to day, addressing themselves

in these words to the Most High. What kingdom is it that they entreat for? Not Christ's
kingdom upon earth, for they are doing much to
stay its progress and hinder its establishment;
and if their wishes could defeat their prayers,
would for ever postpone his coming to possess
it. Or if his kingdom in heaven be intended,
we scarcely think they are so willing or so well
prepared as to renew their entreaties day by day
with heartfelt earnestness. Nay, why need I inquire of another's meaning, I myself have said
it often without knowing or caring what I meant,
without meaning anything. It is an awful thing
to come so solemnly and frequently before Almighty God, and ask we know not what. There
could scarcely perhaps be a better test of our
preparedness for the holy communion than this
one sentence of the Lord's Prayer—" Thy kingdom come." " The kingdom of God is within
you," saith our Lord. As a personal prayer,
we need not make a distinction between the
kingdoms of grace and glory; they are in fact
but a continuance of the same reign within us,
and the one can never be without the other: if
Christ does not reign in our hearts by faith, we
can never be partakers of a more glorious kingdom, whether on earth or in heaven; and He
will not prove so powerless a king, as to lose in
glory the subjects of his grace. We ask, therefore, that his power come within us, that it reign
over us, that it grow in us, and subdue us, and

control us, and do all that sovereignty can do and has a right to do, and graciously wills to do in the disposal of us; until every usurper in our bosoms be expelled, especially the sin that has had dominion over us; all that is opposite, as well as all that opposes itself to the entire subjugation of our souls to his most Holy Spirit. We ask the new birth unto righteousness—for "except a man be born again he cannot see the kingdom of God." "The unrighteous cannot inherit the kingdom." We ask all the discipline, the suffering, it may be, the contempt and persecution by which the children of God are separated from the world, for "We must through much tribulation enter into the kingdom of heaven." We ask to enjoy the highest fruition of the life of faith—"For the kingdom of God is righteousness, and peace, and joy in the Holy Ghost." And daily we repeat the prayer, because we require the perpetual exercise and increase of his sovereign grace within us, as we require the protection of his sovereign power without us; and because on the entire subjugation of our will and affections, and the expulsion of every thing inimical, depends our preparation for the kingdom of heaven, and final attainment of it. It is in short, a prayer for salvation, in all its bearings: personal, individual salvation; with all its blessings, its duties, and its claims; its present peace, and everlasting wealth. And it is a social as well as personal prayer, for the glory of God as well as the salvation of mankind. A time will be "when the kingdoms of this world shall become the kingdoms of our God," and when "He shall judge the quick and dead at his appearing and kingdom;" "When they shall gather out of the kingdom all things that offend;" and the Son of man, the victim heretofore, and now the victor, shall reign alone until his enemies be made his footstool. Consciously or unconsciously; willingly or unwillingly; whatever views we have adopted of the time and manner of our Lord's appearing to establish his universal kingdom, we do indeed invoke that final consummation every time we repeat the prayer. How little expected, how much less desired! "Blessed are they that shall eat bread in the kingdom of heaven;"—that "shall eat and drink at his table in his kingdom, and sit with him on his throne;" but how can I eat the bread of his kingdom upon earth, if I be not ready for the marriage-supper of the Lamb? or how be prepared for that, if I am unfit for this? The communion is but that feast begun; Jesus eats bread with me now in all the sympathy of his suffering manhood; as hereafter I shall eat with him in all the glory of his triumphant Godhead. The slave is weary of his bondage—the oppressed is weary of his oppressor—the captive is weary of his dungeon and his chains—even so longs my soul after thee, O God; and so shall my prayer be, that in me and around me, and for ever the prince of this world be dethroned, and the reign of sin be ended.

I do beseech thee, O King of Kings, by thy long-suffering goodness and protracted promise, now to put forth thy power and come among us. Come in thy grace to them that know thee not: come in more near communion to them that love thee: come, in the season appointed of the Father, and take full possession of thine own. So establish thou now thy throne in my heart, that I may with joy abide the day of thy coming, and stand in my place when thou appearest. Make thyself room by casting out whatever disputes thy power—whatever rivals thy love, or resists thy grace, or divides thy sovereignty within me. Grant, O Lord Jesus, that as the symbols of thy death and resurrection are this day exhibited before me, I may find in them the blessed assurance of my own death unto sin, and resurrection unto life—that dying with thee, and alive unto thee, I may live from day to day in patient desire of thy returning, and most blessed expectation to reign with thee in glory everlasting. Amen.

"THY WILL BE DONE ON EARTH AS IT IS IN HEAVEN."

In Christ only has the will of God been manifested, and in Christ fulfilled; in him exhibited, and in him obeyed; in his example learned, and in his spirit loved, and in his strength attained. Do we ask impossibilities? No; the Father's will has once been done on earth, as perfectly as ever it was done in heaven; done in the likeness of the flesh, and it shall be so again; the enemy has sown tares, but another's scythe shall reap them. "When he shall appear, we shall be like him, for we shall see him as he is." When the blessed Jesus dictated these words, it was as if he enforced his own sayings. "I came not to do mine own will, but the will of my Father which sent me." "If any man will come after me, let him take up his cross daily, and follow me." That conformity to the image of the Son, to which the children of God are predestinated, whether to be made "Conformable to his death, that we may attain to his resurrection," or to be "Transformed by the renewing of our minds, that we may prove what is that good, and acceptable, and perfect will of God," is the personal blessing intreated for in this petition. Is it a hard saying—is it a compulsory prayer;—something that I must say, and ought to wish, and cannot attain to! If I

think so, I have forgotten how my prayer began:
the heavenly Father never willed any thing
inimical to the happiness of his children: and I
have forgotten how he has dealt with me hitherto, for surely goodness and mercy have followed
me all the days of my life: and I have forgotten
his promise, "It is your father's good pleasure
to give you the 'kingdom." If his will were
wholly done on earth, there would be heaven
here: if it were done in me, a child of earth, as
Jesus did it, it would be my heaven. And since
God cannot require impossibilities, or command
a prayer that shall never be fulfilled, it will be
so. The unruly wills and affections of his people shall be conformed, and the opposing wills
of his enemies defeated, and wherever his kingdom is, there shall his will be done. As often
as I repeat this prayer, I seek my own felicity
in time and in eternity; I desire life, security
and peace; I ask to follow Jesus, to death, to
life, to immortality, to be with him, to be like
him; for so is it the Father's will, "In bringing
many sons to glory, to make the captain of
their salvation perfect." If there be one prayer
among many prayers, that can be said with all
my heart, without fear, without reserve, it should
be this: since in it I put myself beyond the reach
of evil, beyond the reach of Satan, the world,
myself, whose adverse willings I have found so
redolent of sorrow, danger, and remorse. When
I consider what his good will has been towards

the sons of men, when He made them in innocence, when He redeemed them in guilt, when
He contrived for them another innocence and
another paradise, his providence, his gifts, his
promises, all that he says He is, and all that I
have found him, the sense of his goodness becomes so overwhelming, I feel as if this should
be my only prayer, "Thy will be done," for I
can want no more. And because I am slow to
learn his will, and weak to do it, and fretful to
submit to it, and wilful to resist it, I will but
repeat my suit the oftener, and urge it the more
vehemently, "Not my will, but thine be done."

PRAYER.

Almighty God, who seest the hearts of all
men, judge me, I pray thee, whether there be
in me any thing that I prefer before thee, and
desire in opposition to thy will, or pursue in
ignorance, or refuse in unbelief: and disclose to
me the secret reservations of my soul, with grace
to put them from me. Make me whatever thou
wouldst have me be—show me what thou
wouldst have me do. It is the desire of my
soul to be conformed in all things to thy will
and pleasure. Enable me to lay upon thy altar
an acceptable gift, myself and all that I have,
the pride of my heart, the wilfulness of my desires, the selfishness of my passions and affec-

20

tions: I desire, O Lord, that they be sacrificed
and put to shame, before these emblems of thy
dying love: thy gentleness, forbearance, meek-
ness, humility, and patient obedience to thy
Father's will. Grant me in these tokens of thy
humanity, so to behold thy perfectness, that I
may love nothing but what thou lovest, and
seek nothing, and choose nothing but in assimi-
lation with thyself; to walk in thy footsteps, to
see thee as thou art, to be with thee, and to be
like thee everlastingly. Amen.

" GIVE US THIS DAY OUR DAILY BREAD."

How beautifully this sentence stands connected with the former, bearing out the Scripture
precept, " Seek first the kingdom of God, and all
these things shall be added unto you." Put
that first which is first, the welfare of the soul,
the desires and necessities of your moral and spiritual existence. And then remember, that he
who made the soul, made the body also. He
does not despise the one half of his work, while
he cherishes the other: he does not treat the
health, and ease, and gratification of our corporeal existence, as things beneath his notice; as
if he were indifferent to its sufferings, and priva-
tions, or would have us insensible to his indulgent provision for it. Jesus had a body as well
as a soul, and he endured bodily wants and

infirmities, as well as mental and spiritual anguish: that he might learn sympathy with both,
and purify and ennoble our whole being, by
taking it into union with himself. True, that
his body was crucified, and so may our's be;
and true, his heart was broken, and so may
our's: but not to condemnation, not to destruction, not abandoned and uncared for by him
who bought us. His body was not left in the
grave; although it was laid there; neither shall
ours be in the dust, though it return thither.—
"The blood of our Lord Jesus Christ, which was
shed for me, preserve my body and soul to everlasting life."

The sentence may comprehend a request for
spiritual, as well as temporal sustentation; all by
which our souls are strengthened and refreshed,
as our bodies are by the bread and wine: but
as it is the only reference in the Lord's prayer
to those temporal blessings which we know we
are to seek of God, I think it was intended by
him in this sense. There was no preference in
the Father's love when He gave his only Son
to assume our whole mortal nature, and render
it all immortal: and He has promised to withhold from neither soul nor body any manner of
thing that is good.

"This day our daily bread;" no doubt intended as an example of the manner in which all
temporal good is to be solicited: with moderate
desires, and limited to the present time. "Be

careful for nothing, but by prayer and supplication make your requests known unto God," "day by day"—our present desires—our daily cares—our existing wants and difficulties, and embarrassments. But make no provision for to-morrow even in your prayers—the morrow can take thought for itself. We have said the prayer to-day, we can say it again to-morrow, and again and again the next day, and " Whatever ye ask, believing, it shall be done unto you." But no forecasting—no anxious and careful anticipations of an uncertain future of which we know nothing, and with which we have nothing to do: if any such prayer be answered, it will be but thus—" Commit yourself to him that careth for you." There will no bonds and securities be given us for the bread of to-morrow, or the independent happiness of years to come. A thought of independence, a feeling of security, would mar this prayer. Whatever my heavenly Father has given me in possession, though it be enough for my life and for my children after me, I will ask it of him every day afresh, for it is not mine for to-morrow: and every day I will receive my earthly blessings as a new grant, fresh from his bountiful hand. Whenever I repeat these words, I intreat He will prolong to me from day to day whatever I would not part with, and add to it what my soul desires or my body needs: whatever the answer be to-day, I would learn to say, "It is well, and let to-morrow be the

secret of omniscience. I do not know, I will
not seek to know what a day may bring forth:
for if I think I do, if I have one day's provision
in my grasp, or one day's independence in my
heart, I cannot say this portion of the prayer; I
cannot mock my Maker with a request for what
I do not want: alas! may I never mock him
with the request of what I cannot trust him for;
distrust, anxiety, will as much spoil my prayer
as independence.

PRAYER.

O thou who hast promised to thy people all
things that are good, and hast never failed in
all the good that thou hast promised;—Thou
who hast called me this day to celebrate the
gift of thy Son, and receive the gifts and
graces of thy Spirit, pardon and put from
me all careful thoughts about the things that
perish, which would unfit me for thy feast—
suppress in me all ambitious and exorbitant
desires, all yearnings of vanity and schemes of
avarice, beyond thy promise of what is needful
for me. O God, thou art the author of all
natural affections, feelings and necessities—to
thee I desire to commit myself for their needful
and wholesome satisfaction, and wait upon thee
in faith for so much of this world's good as will
keep my body from suffering, and my mind

20*

from care. Enable me to appear joyfully at
thy table, in expectation of the good gifts of
thy providence and grace, not according to my
deserts, but according to the measure of thy
great goodness, and the merits of our Lord and
Saviour, Jesus Christ. Amen.

"FORGIVE US OUR TRESPASSES, AS WE FORGIVE THEM THAT TRESPASS AGAINST US."

Penitence and resentment cannot be in exercise in the same bosom at the same time; a deep,
humiliating sense of our own wrong, self-abasement and contrition, cannot co-exist with an
angry and impatient recollection of the wrong
of others: because, however injurious and offensive another's conduct may have been, the
penitent knows secrets of himself that will sink
him lower than any thing he knows of others:
the chief of sinners will see all other sins
eclipsed by the blackness and darkness of his
own. If he does not, if the sense of his own
guilt does not soften his heart to pity and indulgence, it is because he has no due appreciation of it, is no penitent, and consequently no
subject for Divine forgiveness. The Gospel
dwells therefore upon this clause of the petition—"For if ye forgive men their trespasses,
your heavenly Father will also forgive you—
but if ye forgive not men their trespasses,

neither will your heavenly Father forgive your trespasses." Not that our remission of some poor hundred pence is to be the price, and equivalent for our cancelled thousands—nor our seventy times seven to be cast into the balance against our need of daily-renewed forgiveness: but because the disposition to forgive is an indispensable evidence of that state of mind to which only forgiveness has been promised—self-condemnation and self-abhorrence. O when the soul is really there, in dust and ashes before God, how little consciousness is there that we have been or could be wronged by any thing: that the foot which should crush us would do us more than right; or that any being owes us any thing but hatred and destruction. All that is opposed to this spirit of self-abasement—all that is high, vindictive, tenacious and exacting, arbitrary, contentious, and intolerant, is at variance with the intent of the petition. In full agreement with it is the divine injunction, " Leave there thy gift, first go and be reconciled to thy brother;" and the church pursues the idea when to faith and repentance she subjoins, as the only qualification for the sacramental feast, that we be in love and charity with all men.

Shall I examine myself before I proceed with my supplication, whether I have fulfilled the condition of it? No—I will go on—I will say as the Apostles did—" Lord, increase our faith."

I will pray, "Lord, forgive us our trespasses,"
and the thought will shame my pride and melt
my heart, and as I proceed to number my
transgressions, to spread them out before him;
to look backward upon God's unanswered
claims, and the many beside God, to whom I
have not been all that I might have been, all
that they justly might have expected of me,
and forward to the remaining conflict with these
my hated, my forgiven sins; surely the supplication will fulfil its own conditions.   I shall
forget that there is any wrong any where but
in my own sinful bosom: myself to God or man
the only debtor.

"Forgive us"—without Christ there is no
forgiveness of sins.   "This is my blood of the
New Testament, which is shed for many for the
remission of sins."   In Christ, there is no more
remembrance of them.   "Their sins and iniquities will I remember no more"—Heb. x. 17.
"The blood of Christ taketh away all sin."
Addressing ourselves to God the Father, who
for the glory of his hallowed name, and by the
exercise of his sovereign will, hath delivered us
from the power of darkness, and translated us
into the kingdom of his dear Son: in whom we
have redemption through his blood, even the
forgiveness of sins: we come with holy confidence from day to day to renew this granted
prayer, and be re-assured that it is granted.
For though, on behalf of his brethren, Christ

has made an end of transgression, and there is
now no condemnation to them that are in him,
the power of sin is still so great within us, that
it is only by daily penitence our hatred of it can
be manifested, and by daily prayer our hearts be
comforted against it by the renewed sense of
pardon. In the spirit of a child to deprecate a
father's anger, and those timely chastisements,
by which his love has superseded the judgments
of his wrath, which it becomes me yet to fear—
"Blessed is he that feareth always;" as soon as
I am conscious of any sin, though it be but the
sudden emotion or momentary thought, with
the name of Jesus in my mind, if not upon my
lips, I ask forgiveness of my Father, lest that
his anger be stirred, though but a little. And
because there are sins unnumbered, of which I
am not conscious, or commit unmindfully, many
times daily I repeat this prayer—"Forgive us
our trespasses;" and in every exhibition of the
one only oblation and atonement for the sins of
the world, I go to seek fresh assurance of the
forgiveness of my own, while I gather a deeper
sense and quicker sensibility of the desert and
hatefulness of sin.

PRAYER.

O Holy Father, my heart is deceitful above
all things, and thou only knowest it:—deepen

in me, I beseech thee, the hatred and the sense
of sin, that with a mourning and a penitent
spirit, in self-knowledge and self-abhorrence, I
may seek the blessing of forgiveness in the
atoning blood of Christ, and taste the amazing
value of his blood shed, and body broken, and
all the benefits exhibited and promised to me in
this Sacrament. Set before me the follies of
my youth, and the sins of my life past, and the
mass of iniquity that is within me, that I may
intreat thy mercy in presence of this most Holy
Sacrifice, and receive in faith these tokens of
forgiveness: so shall they indeed be precious to
my soul. With thy Spirit's help I do purpose
to render to every man, O blessed Jesus, according as thou hast rendered unto me, mercy, forbearance, and indulgence; to bear with sinners
as thou hast borne with me; and do unto all
men not according to their righteousness, but
after the example of thy loving kindness and
sympathy for the guilty and the unthankful.
Oh pour on me this day, O Lord, the softening
influences of thy Spirit, to subdue the asperities
of my nature, into the likeness of thy love.
Amen.

"LEAD US NOT INTO TEMPTATION, BUT DELIVER
US FROM EVIL."

"Let no man say when he is tempted, I
am tempted of God: for God cannot be tempt-

ed with evil, neither tempteth he any man;
but every man is tempted when he is drawn
away of his own lust and enticed.   Then when
lust hath conceived, it bringeth forth sin; and
sin, when it is finished, bringeth forth death."
Against this process, therefore, I 'conceive it is
that we beseech our heavenly Father, the guide
of our steps, and disposer of our destiny, that
he will in his providence lead us, and by his
grace prevent whatever would prove a temptation to our souls, by the inciting and enticing of
our ungodly passions.   True as it is, and must
be, that God is never the author of the sin
within us, He may for our humiliation and better knowledge of ourselves, afford occasion for
its development, as a skilful mediciner will sometimes provoke a crisis, the better to effect a cure;
and it may be with ourselves to make this necessary, or by timely supplication not so.   He
led his people forty years through the wilderness, to try them, and to prove them, and to
show them what was in their hearts.   And such
I apprehend to be the nature of the evils and
temptations against which we are here instructed to pray.   How many grievous lusts and bitter punishments, timely and honest prayer might
have saved to that rebellious host, is not revealed; but there is no limit to the power of prayer:
he who has undertaken to bring us to the promised land, has not laid down the chart by
which we are to travel thither; there may be

longer ways, and shorter—perilous ways, and
safe ones; ways of darkness through which we
shall be saved, though so as by fire, and ways
of light and peace in which we may almost anticipate our heaven; and this may, I believe I
need not hesitate to say it will, depend upon the
truth and sincerity with which the child of God
can thus address his Father. "Lead us not into
temptation, but deliver us from evil."

Remark the words, for it is no common prayer: and no thing of course that we desire what
we ask. To use it rightly, there needs a heart
more afraid of sin than of any thing beside;
more careful to avoid it, than to possess the
world;—for that world itself, in all the blazon-
ment of its prosperity, its pleasures, and its
smiles, will be oftener than any thing the temptation against which we pray: and the evil of
all evils, temporal and eternal, that we have to
deprecate, is to be partakers in its destinies, and
share its condemnation. Oh no, believe it, it is
no easy prayer to use, in confiding ignorance
of what it may imply. The temptation that
would awake the dormant lust, may lie conceal-
ed in some sweet syren spot, on which our eye
is set for happiness, or hidden in some deep mine
of gold, in which we are about to dig for treasure. Grace has done much indeed for the
heart that can pray daily, at all costs, at all
ventures, "Lead us not into temptation:—
Grant me the refusal of my heart's desires:—

Grant,me the privation of my bosom's treasures. How am I prepared for such dark paradox as may be hidden beneath my daily supplication to be kept from evil, from sin, and all the punishments that follow sin, the only real evils? I be-- lieve it is not without reason that these two sentences are joined in one. Were it what are called the common ills of life that are intended, the two petitions might have stood apart. But in fact, the casualties of life are not, properly speaking, evils to the child of God: thousands shall fall beside him, and ten thousand at his right hand, and it shall not come nigh him, until the moment when his sin provokes, or his purification requires the infliction. We do not pray, nor are we encouraged to pray, that wilfully exposing ourselves to temptation in the gratification of our desires, we may be kept from the spiritual evil that might ensue upon it, or the temporal evil that might bring us to repentance; eternal destruction would be the grant of such a prayer. I ask first—and be it by his grace the first desire of my soul—to be kept from all occasions, opportunities, and incitements to sin: "Lead us not into temptation:" and then, from the evils which my enemies may devise, to do me hurt, or my Father in heaven permit, to do me good, I pray in submission to his wisdom to be relieved, and safely and speedily to be delivered. "Deliver us from evil." Never could I venture to reverse the prayer—to ask a danger-

21

ous and unsanctified prosperity, a preservation from suffering to go on in sin.

Almighty God, who seest that I know not what is good for me, nor how to ask any thing as I ought, hear my prayer according to thy wisdom and goodness, and answer it not according to my ignorance and folly. Give me to dread no evil so much as sin, and to call nothing good but what has thy blessing in it. Enable me, I implore thee, to renounce all sinful pleasures and dangerous pursuits, and ungodly associations and unrighteous gains: which do begin in temptation and end in evil. Grant, Heavenly Father, that as I this day claim the privilege of thy child, and present myself at thy table as a member of Christ, I may come resolved to fulfil the vow that I have taken upon me, to renounce the works of darkness, the pomps and vanities of the world, the lusts of the flesh and the pride of life, and whatever might hinder the divine life within me, or prevent its sacred influence around me. If I am not able of myself to put away the right hand or the right eye that offend; do thou in mercy, O God, remove the evil from me, and give me grace to understand what thou doest, and to praise thy name in all things: in the strength and faith of Jesus, who gave up himself to destroy the works of darkness. Amen.

"FOR THINE IS THE KINGDOM, THE POWER AND
THE GLORY, FOR EVER AND EVER. AMEN."

Independence is the fondest dream of human
imbecility, the maddest project of created being.
Angels conceived it, and were cast out of heaven, for there it could not exist. Man aspired
to it, and was ejected from his Maker's presence,
for there it was impossible. And now in every
fallen soul the in-born desire to be our own, and
not His who made us, is too strong for any thing
but grace to overcome, and even that but
slowly. If we cannot displace the Almighty
from his throne, we would share it with him: or
if we must consent that he should reign in heaven, we will aim at some control in sublunary
things: or if we must give up the kingdom of his
providence, we will be sharers with him in the
kingdom of his grace: to the latest moment we
will have something, be something, do something, of which the power and the praise shall
be our own. So pertinaciously and step by step
do we defend the strong holds of our pride and
independence, that it is not a small thing to find
that point in our Christian course, at which we
can say truly, and with all our heart, "Thine is
the kingdom, the power and the glory," and
add to it our willing and well-pleased "Amen."

It is one aim of the religion of Jesus Christ to
put an end to this conflict between the Creator

and the creature: and the Gospel being the
scheme of God, while all other religions have
been of man's devising, as might be expected,
it is the only one by which boasting is excluded—
" By the law of works?" says the Apostle, " No,
but by the law of faith;" and man is taught, required—nay, compelled to disclaim not his possessions only, but himself;—" Ye are not your
own, ye are bought with a price;"—not only
his bodily and mental powers, but the virtues of
his natural disposition, and all the gifts and
graces of his spiritual life; to renounce every
good thought and right desire, as well as every
work acceptable to God, and give the praise and
glory to another, even to Jesus Christ, who
worketh in us to will and to do according to his
good pleasure:—thus leaving to the fallen sons
of Adam, sin, misery, and death, their sole pro-
prietorship. " Every good gift and every perfect gift is from above, and cometh down from
the Father of lights." Am I content? For if
there is one godly disposition more indispensable
than every other to the due receiving of the
Lord's Supper, it is this renunciation of myself
into the hands of my Redeemer, content to be
nothing, that He may be all; to be abased, that
He may be exalted; to be counted among those
that were lost, that He may have all the glory
of my salvation. Yes, Lord, I am content.—
Were I less fallen, I never could have known
such love as thine: I never could have seen all

I now see in those precious emblems of thy body and blood, or tasted such sweetness while I feed upon thee in them; surely I never could have loved thee as I do. "Thine be the kingdom, the power, and the glory." Every fresh discovery of my dependence is but a new security for my salvation: the sense of it is my present peace, the knowledge of it my best assurance of happiness for ever. I desire to be independent only of myself and rest my all on thee. The Father hath given all power to the Son: the representative of Jehovah upon earth—the Word; the incarnate Word, that in the beginning was with God, and was God: by whom all things were made—in whom is Life. Jesus is my Saviour, my brother, my beloved; who else should have dominion over me—to whom else would I commit the power, or ascribe the glory? One with the Father and the Holy Spirit, I believe him to be true and very God; and as I believe, so from my soul I do desire, "Thine be the kingdom, the power, and the glory, for ever and ever." Amen and Amen.

PRAYER.

Forasmuch as thou hast required, O thou just and holy God, that all who approach thy sacred feast, should renounce themselves, and all that is their own, and all that they have done, and of

21*

thy free grace accept the benefits to be received thereby;—so bless me with the sense of my dependence, as having nothing, and yet possessing all things; nothing in myself, but all things in Christ my Saviour, that I may desire all glory to be given him in heaven and earth, and thank thee, O Father, that thou hast laid on him the salvation and government of all. Make it the choice of my heart to be nothing, that I may owe all things to his love; to come naked, that I may be clothed with his righteousness; hungry, that I may feed upon his flesh and blood; poor, that I may subsist upon the riches of his grace; helpless, and lost, and miserable, that I may rejoice for ever in the song of heaven—"Blessing, and honor, and glory, and power, be unto him that sitteth on the throne, and unto the Lamb for ever and ever." Amen.

SACRAMENTAL THOUGHTS.

SACRAMENTAL THOUGHTS.

"FOR AS OFTEN AS YE EAT THIS BREAD, AND DRINK THIS CUP, YE DO SHEW THE LORD'S DEATH TILL HE COME."—1 Cor. xi, 26.

"Till he come"—"And they shall look on me whom they have pierced; and they shall mourn for him as one mourneth for his only son." Zech. xii, 10. And if they must, how little does it avail us to refuse, to be unwilling, to be unready, or even to be afraid, to behold him now. When those rocks and hills that we shall invoke to hide us, will only reverberate our long refusal; when He who hath stretched forth his hand and no man regarded, shall laugh at our calamity and mock our fears; when the cry of the bridegroom breaks in upon our unfitness, and finds us and leaves us in eternal darkness; is it then we shall be more ready, more willing, less afraid? If not, there is but little time to lose. The first watch and the second watch are past; what must be at some time, may be at any time. "The world passeth away and the fashion thereof." But what is time, or what is earth to me? I have no time but the moment

that my present pulsation numbers; no earth
but the space I stand upon; the next step may
find no footing here, "Every eye shall see him,
and they that pierced him," and they that reject
him, and they that forget him. Yes, and they
that fear him, if, before his coming, fear be not
cast out by perfect love. If we are any such, it
does not become us to lie down this night in
peace; in safety we cannot lie. Unworthy or
unwilling to look upon the figurative emblems
of the Saviour's death and passion, emblems of
patience, lowliness, and sorrow; how shall we
bear to look upon Himself;—" when he shall be
revealed from heaven with his mighty angels,
taking vengeance on them that know not God,
and that obey not the Gospel of our Lord Jesus
Christ." Blessed Redeemer! I had better meet
thee now, unworthy though I am, and fearful
and ashamed, and know thee in thy humiliation,
before I meet thee in thy glory. There is in thee
a remedy for unworthiness, for fear and shame;
but there is none for the refusal of thyself.

"Shall look on him and mourn;" "Blessed
are they that mourn," mourn now, "for they
shall be comforted;" weep like the believing
women at the grave of the crucified, until they
find him in the risen God: or like Mary, when
in ignorance and doubt, she went to seek the
living among the dead, and wept because she
found him not, or knew not it was He.
Blessed in ignorance, doubtfulness, and tears,

are they that mourn now the crucified Jesus, and seek him sorrowing at the cross and in the tomb. He is not there, but presently he will reveal himself, in all the blessings and benefits of his resurrection unto life eternal. If we be dead with him, we shall also live with him. Stranger though I be to his encouraging and peace-speaking voice, I may go with my sorrow, my ignorance and unbelief, while there is yet in Him a pardon and a comforter provided. But who will comfort them that never weep till the time of rejoicing comes, and never look on Him whom they have pierced, till they behold him in the Lord of glory; outcast mourners of a rejoicing universe, destined to look— to look for ever from the bottomless pit of their perdition, upon Him whom they first slew, and then rejected. Lamb of God, Son of God, let me know thee first in thy humanity, the terrors of the Deity put off—the man of sorrows, the willing sacrifice, the suffering, uncomplaining, unreproaching victim. Let me wait beneath thy cross, go down into thy tomb, ask where they have laid thee, and weep until I find thee; drink in these elements of the bitterness of thy cup, and be baptised with thy baptism unto death;—that so at thy second coming I may be found as those that are alive from the dead, over whom the second death hath no power.

"Pierced." Who pierced him? Not the chaplet of thorns, nor the heathen soldier's spear;

nor the Jewish Caiaphas, nor the Roman Pilate; nor even he who dipped his hand with him in the dish. "Behold, I lay down my life, no man taketh it from me." *They* slew him who brought him down from heaven to die; whose iniquities hid from him his Father's face; whose mortal miseries broke his guiltless heart; and theirs the deepest wound, who would not let him save them. He prayed for his murderers, he only wept for these; they slew his manhood, for they knew him not; these slay as it were the very Deity that they deny—"Crucify to themselves the Son of God afresh, and put him to open shame:"—those were forgiven, these can never be so.

And now I could think my wrong is deeper still. I pierced him, and mine was the deepest thrust of all, for I am convinced that he was God. I know that he came down to seek and to save the lost—to save me; to give himself a ransom for sinners—for me, the chief of sinners. I am persuaded of all that he endured, and all that he has done to procure salvation for us, and all that he still does to bring us to it. I do not question the truth of this narration, nor doubt the reality of this mysterious transaction. This and much more, oh how much more—I know, of the love of Him who died! and yet I will not go to him—I am afraid to trust him—I shun his presence, and neglect his ordinances, and refuse him what he died for—the salvation of my soul. "Deny the Lord that bought them" —deny him his own, withhold from him of the travail of his soul that he may be satisfied. If we know how hard it is to bear unkindness in return for love; to be repulsed with doubts, and requited with suspicions, and answered with refusals where we have rendered all; if we know, and who does not know? how deep the wound may be of ill-requited benefits, and wronged affection, we need not be in doubt who pierced the Holy One; who wove the sharpest thorn into his crown, and threw the bitterest herb into his cup. I did it—I, who at this moment hesitate to accept his offers of salvation, to believe his promises and trust his love, and take his holy sacrament to my great and endless comfort—I, who, when he bids me to his supper, make excuses, refuse to go, or go mistrustful, or return unthankful—more blessed in the forgetfulness than the remembrance of Him.

"Behold, I come quickly." It is in vain to put the prediction from us: a thousand years are but as yesterday when it is passed. The kingdom of heaven is at hand, and "Except a man be born again, he cannot see the kingdom of God." "Except ye eat the flesh of the Son of man, and drink his blood, ye have no life in you." Unless we be partakers, not of the outward and visible sign only, but of the inward and spiritual grace of both the Holy Sacraments, we have no participation in his death and resur-

22

rection, and how shall we "abide the day of his coming, or stand when he appeareth." Unwelcome first when he came as a stranger to his own—"riding upon an ass, and a colt the foal of an ass," "and lifted not up his voice in the streets, nor broke the bruised reed, nor quenched the smoking flax;" unwelcome now when he comes into the sanctuary, crowned with the rainbow wreath of promise, in his hand the olive-branch of peace, and thrones himself upon his altar, to distribute the gifts and graces of his Spirit; once slain, and twice rejected, what will the welcome of his kingdom be, when crowned with the jewels that his blood has purchased, the sword of recompence in his hand, and the day of vengeance in his heart—"He cometh with clouds, and every eye shall see him, and they also which pierced him, and all kindreds of the earth shall wail because of him?" Before we refuse, before we say we are unfit, or afraid to meet him at his table, let us consider the alternative, we must behold him, no distant, invisible, inaccessible deity, but "the Son of Man, seated at the right hand of power," "That same Jesus whom ye crucified, both Lord and Christ." The Jesus whom we have pierced, the Christ whom we have neglected, is the God and Lord whom we must look upon, face to face. Shall we go on, and say we are afraid? afraid to remember what we are not afraid to forget; afraid to trust, but not to disobey him? Oh, would we were afraid, for there is cause—to behold the coming, not the departing Lord—to brave the living, not the dying Saviour. Mark the contrast—"Look unto me, all ye ends of the earth, and be ye saved." "They shall look upon him whom they have pierced, and mourn."

"As a thief in the night."—This night—any night—in the body or out of the body, Jesus, Son of God, I may be with thee before thy throne, or be an outcast for ever from the kingdom of thy grace or glory!

There is no time to lose; the bread of life, the blood of reconciliation is offered me to-day. All things are ready except myself. It may be too late, it cannot be too soon, that I determine to draw near unto thee, and take of what thy gracious hand holds out. Oh give me grace to know what I should do to-day, for I have no to-morrow. Prepare my heart, or take it unprepared; call me, unworthy and unwilling, from these paths of indifference and indecision, and by the power of thy Spirit compel me to come in before the doors be closed on me for ever, and to all that I have done against thee, to the sin that has crucified and the unbelief that has rejected thee, there be added this last, this only inexpiable wrong—the refusal of thy latest invitation.

"BEHOLD I COME QUICKLY."—Rev. xxii, 12.

Wilt thou return
Thou great, thou distant One!
On clouds of heaven
Triumphant lighting down?

Shall I see thee
Thou loved now unseen!
Thy manhood clothed
In deity serene?

See thee, my God,
My Saviour, brother, friend!
And be with thee
Where visits never end!

Or here, or there—
Be it at thy decree—
I know no heaven
Except the sight of thee.

If I e'er try
To think what heaven is—
Its pearly gates,
Its golden seats of bliss—

Nor form, nor mould
To fancy's search is given,
And answer none
But "Jesus is thy heaven."

Blessed Saviour!
Thou art my heaven now—
Fountain of joy
Whence all its currents flow.

Musing thy word
I hear thy voice the while—

On nature's front
I see thy loving smile—

Upon my knees
I seem to know thee near—
　Thy table spread,
I feel that thou art there:

And when I share
Its hallowed mystery,
　In tasted love
My spirit feeds on thee.

So known, so seen,
In sweet communion near,
　In sympathy
So holy and so dear;

Jesus, I think,
Thus, communing with thee,
　Yes, I can think
What heaven perhaps may be.

My bosom swells.
To give thy presence room—
　Come, Lord Jesus,
O quickly, quickly come!

CONTEMPLATION OF THE ELEMENTS.

"GO AND PREPARE US THE PASSOVER, THAT WE MAY EAT."

Emblems of ill
Blest harbingers of weal,
In these mysterious treasures of thy board
Eternal Lord!
Thyself reveal.

22*

Thyself, as on the eve
    Of that last fearful leave
Thou wert to take, thou sat'st the saddest guest
    At thine own feast,
The most unwelcomed and the most unblest;
    Thyself all sympathy, all love,
But not in earth beneath or heaven above,
One kindred soul, one heart participant
To echo thee thy solitary plaint.
Would that my faith could reach thee, blessed One!
Not as thou art upon thy throne,
    God incomprehensible,
        Invisible,
    Beyond the stretch,
    Beyond the longing reach
        Of mortal imbecility,
To share thy nature, or to dwell with thee:—
    No—I would think thee as thou wert, a man—
Infinitude diminished to the span
Of man's affections—something
    That I can bring,
As like to like, within the little sphere
Of sympathies and sweet communion near,
Which only kindred souls with kindred share.
    Let the dark heathen serve his unknown God,
    And wisdom proud
    Be thankless for the mystery of thy birth,
    A child of earth—
I love—O how I love to gaze on thee,
Thou soften'd beam of light's intensity!—
So pure, and yet so mild! As when
Upon the darkness of this globe terrene
The morning sun obtrudes himself, not hastily,
Quenching our vision with the blaze of day;
But with a mellowed flame
Seen first unfelt—the same,

And yet how different, that presently
Will drive his blazing chariot through the sky,
 O'er each averted eye—
Now walking forth so harmlessly,
 So seeming nigh,
Fancy could almost think to clasp his zone
And scatheless take him for her own.
 Ride on, thou risen God, and on the head
Of these thy creatures, from thy zenith shed,
The fructifying day-beams of thy grace,
Meridian treasures of thy heavenly place.
The time will be when I shall love thee so,
 But now
Used to night,
I love to gaze on the attempered light
Of thy pale rising o'er the slumbering earth,
Sight fitter for an eye of this world's birth.
I love to call thee Jesus—love to dwell,
 Blessed Immanuel,
Without that wide infinitude between,
That chilling secrecy of things unseen,
Upon thy mortal form—on thee, a man—
 One
Who felt as I feel, loved as I have loved;
 Was moved
To prayers, to tears, to sighs, even as I,
Respondent language of infirmity,
The brother, husband, friend, whate'er
 On earth is dear—
All that I ever loved—and Oh, how far above
 All I have had to love,
Seemest thou thus to me, and still my Lord,
My Saviour and my God.
And here, O Jesus, in thy holy place,
 Attent upon thy grace,

I come to gaze
  Upon the mystery
That tells me thou couldst dief
  And with a dying one
  On heaven's high throne
    Canst share
The earth-wak'd sorrow, and the earth-shed tear,
  And canst divide with me
Earth's worst and weariest—even with me
    The bliss of thine eternity.

PRAYER.

LORD Jesus, Son of God and Son of man, as
by the taking of my nature into thine, thou art
become partaker of all my susceptibilities and
infirmities, and by my spiritual union with thee
hast made me capable of participating in all thy
glories, and perfections, grant, I beseech thee,
that I may no more have or desire to have any
separate existence, any thought or feeling or faculty independent of thee; any possessions but
in use for thee, any loves but what thou lovest,
or grief or pleasure such as thou wilt share with
me—or cares, but such as I may cast upon thee.
Grant, Lord, that as I now take into my corporeal frame these emblems of thy humanity, to
nurture, and sustain, and become incorporate in
it, so may I imbibe and take into my soul, the
light, and life, and holiness of thy divine nature
and grow upon it day by day into thy more per-

fect likeness, till I become pleasing as thou art
in the Father's sight, and meet to sit down with
thee in the kingdom of thy glory, as thou thyself hast sat down in the kingdom of thy Father. Amen.

A PENITENT'S PRAYER.

BLESSED Jesus, ever near and ever present
God, look, I beseech thee, into the close places
of my soul, and behold its hidden anguish. I
would hide nothing from thee. Thou hast
known what it is to look for pity and there was
none for comforters but there was no man. Oh
by the anguish of thy soul that night have pity
on my sorrows, and forgive my iniquity, for it is
very great. Thou only knowest how great it
is, and only thou canst behold me without abhorrence. Men could not bear, angels could
not bear to see what thou seest; how can I look
into myself and live? Against thee, thee only
have I sinned—against thy light and against
thy love; against all that I have seen, and known
and felt of thy amazing goodness. My Lord
and my God, I have crucified thee, and put thee
to shame, and chosen Barabbas before thee in
my heart: the sin, the murderous sin for the love
of which I have dishonored and disowned thee.
On me be the shame, O Lord. I am contented

to be vile and base, and abominable as I am, if
only thou wilt get thee glory upon my shame,
and save me from myself, from the bondage of
this corruption. Thou God seest me, where I
am; and thou hearest what they say, " God has
forsaken him, persecute him, and take him, for
there is none to deliver him." Shall thine enemies have the triumph? Shall they carry off the
spoil from under the shadow of thy cross? I lay
myself, I leave myself in the dust before thee.
I come this day to thy altar, sinful, polluted, and
ashamed; and bring all my guilt and all my
misery with me, to try if it is beyond thy mercy
and exceeds the value of thy most precious
blood. I fix my eyes upon the emblems of thy
death and passion, and gaze in thought upon the
serpent as it was lifted up in the wilderness; in
the midst of them that had provoked thee, and
denied thee, and hardened their hearts, and made
to themselves other gods, as I have; if perhaps
I may be healed as they were. Lord, thou
knowest all things, thou knowest that I hate the
sin that has bound its scorpion folds about me,
hand and foot, till I have no power or strength
against it. Yet speak but the word, touch but
with thy breath these bonds of my affliction, and
they will fall away, like the thread of tow when
it touches the fire. Lord, speak thou from thine
altar this day, and say to my soul, " Go and sin
no more."

" IF ANY MAN SIN, WE HAVE AN ADVOCATE WITH THE FATHER,
JESUS CHRIST THE RIGHTEOUS, AND HE IS THE PROPITIATION
FOR OUR SINS."

THRONED Saviour, risen Lord,
  Behold a brother's tears,
Far from thy Father's presence hear,
  A banish'd brother's prayers.

It was but a look of thine,
  One look of love the same,
That brake the false apostle's heart,
  And brought him back to shame.

O turn that melting look on me,
  And break this bosom's frost;
An Adam fall'n a second time,
  A prodigal twice lost.

In vain I taste thy hallowed bread,
  And see thy wine outflow;
Sweet emblems heretofore of love,
  Mementoes now of woe.

Press'd now between unhallowed lips,
  Touch'd by a hand profane,
I see thy falling manna round,
  And gather it in vain.

I cannot take, I cannot eat,
  Nor call thee now mine own,
Unfaithfulness has seared my heart,
  And sinned it into stone.

But one blest look of thine could break,
  This heart's impenitence,
One day-beam of reviving love,
  Would drive the coldness hence.

O Jesus, turn and look on me,
That look so loved, so known,
As I was used to see thee once,
Thy blest and faithful one.

And these sweet pledges of thy love,
Not always pledged in vain,
O let thy grieved Spirit come,
And speak in them again.

And take thine own, and find thy lost,
And claim thy rifled gem,
And get thee honor for thyself,
Upon a brother's shame.

PRAYER.

Blessed Lord, since it has pleased thee to spread thy table, and exhibit before our eyes the sacred emblems of thy cross and passion, and all that thou hast done and suffered for us; give us, we beseech thee, clearly to see, and duly to appreciate all the benefits to be received thereby. Give us to realise our mysterious union with thee, and feed upon thee in our hearts, while we eat this bread, and drink this cup to our great and endless comfort. By the witness of thy Holy Spirit, by the verity of thy sacred word, by thy own sensible presence in our souls, certify to us, Holy Saviour, blessed Master, what it is to be one with thee, in the unity of the Spirit, in the bond of peace, and in righteousness of life. As we press that bread between our teeth, give us to know that we were in thee, when thy body was broken; as we wet our lips with that hallowed cup, give us to realise the fact, that we died with thee when thy blood flowed out;—died to sin, to misery, to hell; died to the law that could not cleanse us, and to the world that could not satisfy us, and to that death itself in all its terrors, which held our souls in bondage. We desire no life, no joy, no being but in thee; we fear no death, but that which would separate us from thee. When we draw near to take thy Holy Sacrament, give us to feel thy vivifying Spirit within, strengthening and refreshing our souls with a blessed assurance, that we are indeed made alive, created anew, born of thy Spirit, risen in thy resurrection, bound up in thy life, over which death hath no more power:—And in the taking of these elements, O Lord our God, sustain the life thou hast imparted, uphold the faith thou hast given, keep our lamps burning, and our souls expecting, until thou come again to be revealed in them whom thou hast chosen, and faith be swallowed up in sight, and hope in joy, and conflict in victory, and victory itself in everlasting peace. Glory be to thee, O God most high.

"IF WE HAVE BEEN PLANTED TOGETHER IN THE LIKENESS OF
HIS DEATH, WE SHALL BE ALSO IN THE LIKENESS OF HIS RESUR-
RECTION."—Rom. vi, 5.

Bound with thorns of mortal sorrow,
As they once thy temples pressed,
Bathed in dews of mental anguish,
As they once suffused thy breast:

Folly-stricken, worn and wearied,
'Neath this sense of misery,
Earth estranged and heaven distant,
Jesus! am I one with thee?

Is this sigh that swells my bosom
One of those that breathed in thee?
Is this heart by sorrow broken,
One with that which broke for me.

If 'twas sin that pierced thy forehead,
If 'twas shame that broke thy heart,
In the likeness of thy dying,
Well were mine a brother's part.

Likeness of thy straitened spirit
Longing for its resting-place:
Likeness of thy bitter crying,
For thy Father's hidden face:

Blessed Jesus! breathe a whisper,
In my list'ning, longing ear;
Witness of thy Holy Spirit,
If it is thy cross I bear.

Base desires crucifying,
Shame and anguish welcome be;
Germ of life and glory coming,
If it likens me to Thee.

"FOR WE BEING MANY ARE ONE BREAD, AND ONE BODY; FOR
WE ARE ALL PARTAKERS OF THAT ONE BREAD."—1 Cor. x,
17.

"THERE SHALL NO SIGN BE GIVEN THEM BUT THE SIGN OF THE
PROPHET JONAS."—Mark iii, 12.

WHEN in that deepest deep
  Hidden from day,
Hidden from all but Thee,
  The prophet lay:

Dead to all sympathy
  From things below,
No more a living one,
  Except in woe:

Didst Thou, O Lord of Life,
  In the dark fold
Of Hell's eternal gates
  Thyself behold!

Thyself in him, the doomed
  The outcast one—
Forth of a sinking world
  In judgment thrown!

Oh! in a deeper deep
  Behold us then—
And in these waters own
  Thyself again.

As counted once for us
  Among the dead—
That ocean weight of guilt
  About thy head:

None to respond to thee
  Or feel, or hear—

Except the Eternal One—
   And He not there;

He deafened to thy cry,
   By the wild roll
Of those mysterious waves
   Upon thy soul.—

By thy remember'd grief
   When thou wert thus;
Oh! blessed Jesus, know
   Thyself in us.

Partakers in thy death,
   And in thy fears—
Oh! count our sorrows thine,
   And thine our tears.

And thine the enemies
   That seek our shame—
To blacken with our guilt
   Thy holy name.

"Ye did it unto me"—
   Repeat that word
Through Hell's malignant host
   Despairing heard.

Say it in earth—in heaven,
   Thy people own—
Oh! say it in our hearts,
   That we are "one."

"THIS DO IN REMEMBRANCE OF ME."

REMEMBRANCE! Is there one on earth
But knows what that may mean,
When spectral images come back,
Of something that has been?

Something that neither time nor tears
Have altered since it was—
How often on a day serene,
There comes a cloud across;

A form, a voice, a countenance,
The spot where deeds were done,
And casts its sackcloth hues athwart
The summer's mid-day sun.

But most—Oh who of sinful mould
But knows what memory is,
When in the dark, deep thinking hours
Of midnight wretchedness,

It stands with its emblazon'd roll,
The only visible,
In its red hand the mixen cup
Of a fore-tasted hell.

Well knew they of the fallen soul
In olden poets' theme,
Who could invent no Paradise
Without a Lethe's stream.

It was for Thee, thou blessed one!
In these sweet pledges given,
It was for Thee alone to make
Of memory's self a heaven.

The hallowed grief, the cancelled guilt,
The love-remitted debt;
Thine is no cold oblivious cup—
We need not to forget.

Oh rather let remembrance be
Our paradise above,
Our whole eternity of bliss
The memory of thy love.

POPULAR BOOKS

RECENTLY PUBLISHED BY

HERMAN HOOKER,

N. W. CORNER OF CHESTNUT AND FIFTH STS.

Blunt's Lectures on the Life of Christ. In 1 vol. 12mo.

Blunt's Lectures on the Life of St. Paul.

Blunt's Lectures on the Life of Abraham and Jacob.

Blunt's Lectures on the Life of St. Peter and the Thirty-nine Articles.

Blunt's Lectures on the Life of Elisha.

Blunt's Lectures on the History of the Seven Churches of Asia.

Blunt's Sermons. 1 vol. Selected by himself.

Henry's Communicant's Companion. By Howard Malcom.

A Book of Family Prayer. By Rev. W. F. Hook, 'D.D.

A Treatise on Prayer. By Rev. Edward Bickersteith.

Harmony of the Four Gospels. By the same Author.

The Life and Opinions of Rev. Dr. Milne, Missionary to China. By Robert Philip.

The Book of Common Prayer, according to the use of the Protestant Episcopal Church. 18mo. Sheep.

The same work. Morocco extra.

Hare's Discourses on the Second Coming of Christ.

Church Dictionary. By Staunton. 2d edition, enlarged.

Flora's Lexicon. By Miss Waterman, (fancy paper.)

The same work. Muslin, extra gilt, four colored plates.

 Trieste

Trieste Publishing has a massive catalogue of classic book titles. Our aim is to provide readers with the highest quality reproductions of fiction and non-fiction literature that has stood the test of time. The many thousands of books in our collection have been sourced from libraries and private collections around the world.

The titles that Trieste Publishing has chosen to be part of the collection have been scanned to simulate the original. Our readers see the books the same way that their first readers did decades or a hundred or more years ago. Books from that period are often spoiled by imperfections that did not exist in the original. Imperfections could be in the form of blurred text, photographs, or missing pages. It is highly unlikely that this would occur with one of our books. Our extensive quality control ensures that the readers of Trieste Publishing's books will be delighted with their purchase. Our staff has thoroughly reviewed every page of all the books in the collection, repairing, or if necessary, rejecting titles that are not of the highest quality. This process ensures that the reader of one of Trieste Publishing's titles receives a volume that faithfully reproduces the original, and to the maximum degree possible, gives them the experience of owning the original work.

We pride ourselves on not only creating a pathway to an extensive reservoir of books of the finest quality, but also providing value to every one of our readers. Generally, Trieste books are purchased singly - on demand, however they may also be purchased in bulk. Readers interested in bulk purchases are invited to contact us directly to enquire about our tailored bulk rates. Email: customerservice@triestepublishing.com

You May Also Like

The Works of James Russell Lowell, Vol. VII. The Poetical Works of James Russell Lowell, in Four Volumes, Vol. I

James Russell Lowell

ISBN: 9780649640430
Paperback: 332 pages
Dimensions: 6.14 x 0.69 x 9.21 inches
Language: eng

Results of Astronomical Observations Made at the Sydney Observatory, New South Wales, in the Years 1877 and 1878

H. C. Russell

ISBN: 9780649692613
Paperback: 120 pages
Dimensions: 6.14 x 0.25 x 9.21 inches
Language: eng

www.triestepublishing.com

You May Also Like

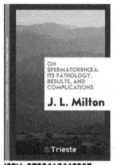

On Spermatorrhœa: Its Pathology, Results, and Complications

J. L. Milton

ISBN: 9780649663057
Paperback: 188 pages
Dimensions: 6.14 x 0.40 x 9.21 inches
Language: eng

Persecution and Tolerance: Being the Hulsean Lectures Preached Before the University of Cambridge in 1893-4

Mandell Creighton

ISBN: 9780649669356
Paperback: 164 pages
Dimensions: 6.14 x 0.35 x 9.21 inches
Language: eng

www.triestepublishing.com

You May Also Like

ISBN: 9780649333158
Paperback: 84 pages
Dimensions: 6.14 x 0.17 x 9.21 inches
Language: eng

Report of the Department of Farms and Markets, pp. 5-71

Various

ISBN: 9780649324132
Paperback: 78 pages
Dimensions: 6.14 x 0.16 x 9.21 inches
Language: eng

Catalogue of the Episcopal Theological School in Cambridge Massachusetts, 1891-1892

Various

You May Also Like

Three Hundred Tested Recipes

Various

ISBN: 9780649352142
Paperback: 88 pages
Dimensions: 6.14 x 0.18 x 9.21 inches
Language: eng

A Basket of Fragments

Anonymous

ISBN: 9780649419418
Paperback: 108 pages
Dimensions: 6.14 x 0.22 x 9.21 inches
Language: eng

Find more of our titles on our website. We have a selection of thousands of titles that will interest you. Please visit

www.triestepublishing.com